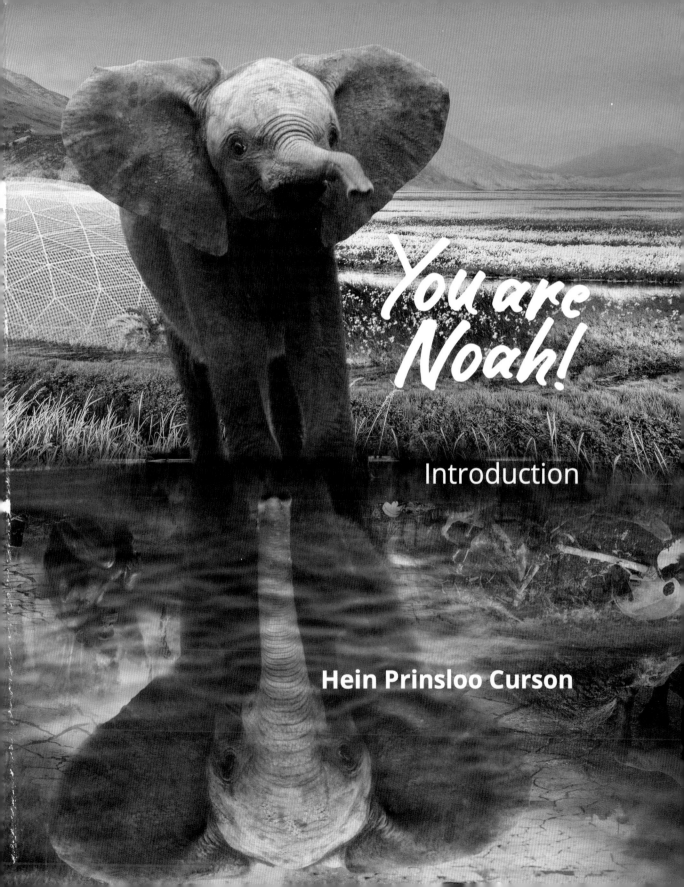

You are Noah!

Introduction

Hein Prinsloo Curson

We would like to thank all of our wonderful corporate supporters who have helped the Noah's Ark project come alive:

Galaxy Forest Lodge

First published 2021
Published by GB Publishing Org
www.gbpublishing.co.uk
Copyright © 2021 Hein Prinsloo Curson
All rights reserved

ISBNs:
978-1-912576-71-5 (hardback)
978-1-912576-72-2 (paperback)
978-1-912576-73-9 (eBook)
978-1-912576-74-6 (Kindle)

Cover Design © 2021 Brett Rory Lipman

PR:
Prinsloo Curson Associates
Jabulani Matobela Consultants (Project Principal)
Claire Barber PR – Noah's Ark PR & Social Media Marketing
Roxanne Smith PR – Jacaranda FM Radio
Mariska van Eeden – Eeden Social Media Marketing with
Emile Van Eeden
Javis Talwar

Photographs – with our gratitude – are from:
Noah's Ark Series 1
Afternoon Express
ENCA
Monique De Paiva – Studio & wildlife photos
Peta-Janice Smith – Bio-diversity photos
Danny Chapters – Jeanique Danté Fourie
AMC – photos from their collection
ITV Studios
nick@nickboulton.com

A catalogue record of the printed book is available from the British Library

Designed and typeset by Evolution Design & Digital Ltd (Kent)

Table of Contents

The Team

Of course setting out to build the biggest conservation project ever, anywhere in the world, is a mammoth undertaking.

Not biggest in area – it doesn't come close to that of the Kavango Zambezi Transfrontier Conservation Area spanning 440,000 square kilometres across African countries.

But it is without doubt the most ambitious yet for the high level of wildlife protection envisioned.

Success will come, each step of the way, with the public behind us – we need every individual in the world who can contribute in the smallest way, even just raising voices – and conservation heroes bringing their enthusiasm and specialist knowledge. The project is off and running, and for that we gathered The Noah's Ark team.

So, let me introduce them:

Figure 1 Noah's Ark Team

MEMBERS and ROLES:

Richard Prinsloo Curson (Richard)	Co-Founder and President
Hein Prinsloo Curson (Hein)	Co-Founder and Vice-President
Polica Kgaugelo Sekhwela (Kgaugelo)	Community Director
Thobekile Ndlovu (Thobe)	Liaison to Royal Tribal Leaders
Christina Mkhabela (Christina)	Woman's Ambassador & Project Leader
Peta-Janice Smith (Peta)	Biodiversity Expert
Tholoana Molapo (Tholo)	Production Manager
Omee Otis (Omee)	Ambassador
Hannatjie Prinsloo (Hannatjie)	Office & Team Manager
Brett Rory Lipman (Brett)	Brand Manager
Claire Barber of Claire Barber PR (Claire)	PR

See Management & Support for the Team's biographies

In memory of His Majesty King Goodwill Zwelithini ka Bhekuzulu, Monarch of The Zulu Kingdom in South Africa

Figure 2

Figure 3 Children remembering animals

Dedication

"To all our children for generations to come
That they shall all know the joy of growing up with animals
Yes, in movies, arts, books, gardens, fields and zoos
But most of all everywhere real and WILD"
Javis Talwar 13, of Malaysia,
Global Youth Ambassador, The Noah's Ark Foundation

Noah's Ark Status
– Leading the World

Noah's Ark leads the world in high-tech conservation for the future.

Conceptual designs and land acquisition are complete, after many weeks, and so now are surveys both from the air and on the ground.

Those brave steps have prepared the way for constructing the 21st Century Noah's Ark, a beacon to preserving the whole of planet Earth for the future.

Every shovel, brick and nail put to building this mega monument to mankind and nature, will be with love, sweat and tears. This is where it all began…

Figure 4 Aerial view of the Noah's Ark area in KwaZulu-Natal, South Africa

THE PROJECT

The World's Biodiversity Crisis

"Over the last century kelp forests have declined by approximately 40% and the biomass of large predatory fishes is now under 33% of what it was."
frontiers in Conservation Science

Figure 5 Climate Change: Wildfires in Australia, Drought in Africa

This planet is dying

There is no denying this planet is dying. Or rather nature is dying, in a mass extinction of prehistoric proportions. The chilling facts are there to follow, in the green circles on early pages.

In a nutshell – market forces have a life of their own, funded by capital, driven by consumer demand, steered by branding, delivered by grass-roots workers. Fair trade, which aims to balance rewards through supply chains, is a humanitarian initiative against inequality. Its success will bring prosperity to developing regions, in turn increasing demand. This then becomes a planetary issue, in that incremental demand raises pressure for land and sea transformation to economic use.

We demand more than the planet's capacity to deliver

The rate of that increase is already unsustainable, the bio capacity level was 1.6 in 2019 (UN data), before factoring in population growth which is also rocketing up. That is, we already demand more than the planet's capacity to deliver and that is worsening with each decade that passes.

It's time to raise your voice with millions of others to say *stop*!

People everywhere must listen, world leaders must listen, all the influencers out there must listen.

It is not impossible. Sure there is fighting, poverty, slavery and death, inequality and injustice. The world came through millennia of suffering culminating in two world wars but the will is now there to put an end to misery. We must get all of that behind us and strive for a more caring world. And we will, just as the world community has acted to combat the COVID-19 pandemic. There has never been a greater example of solidarity on that scale.

We can and we will prevail in keeping nature with us. Accords are building to not only allocate but also protect more and more territories from exploitation. It is targeted to keep as much as 30%, many argue for 50%, as wildernesses. More troubling is the wildlife of those territories. As their natural habitats dwindle their numbers become greater in captivity and, especially once made extinct, can never be brought back.

Figure 6 Climate Change: A Tiger in India

Figure 7 Plastic pollution in the ocean

"Population sizes of vertebrate species have declined by an average of 68% over the last five decades, with certain population clusters in extreme decline, presaging the imminent extinction of their species," frontiers in Conservation Science, Jan 2021

Figure 8 Plastic pollution in wildlife

"The number of animals living on the Earth has plunged by half since 1970. The number of tigers has plunged by 97% in the last century."
The Guardian 2018

Figure 9 Biodiversity Crisis, Noah's Ark on Afternoon Express (ZA)

Land occupied by indigenous communities holds 80% of Earth's biodiversity

That is why preserving wildernesses together with their natural inhabitants is of the utmost importance. And, the best way to achieve that – given that "the quarter of Earth's land now owned, used or occupied by indigenous communities holds about 80% of Earth's biodiversity" – is to save endangered species by "empowering indigenous groups to manage their lands". That initiative, coupled with changing the culture of the outside world to want that, is what non-profit The Noah's Ark Foundation is about.

Loving nature with fun and excitement in our hearts

And we can do all of that by loving nature with fun and excitement in our hearts. In the end, saving The Noah's Ark TV series has that aim, by cultivating widespread community engagement through music and uplifting themes of transforming lives locally, promoting cross-Africa collaboration and building vital international partnerships.

A high-security conservation park for endangered species

The concept is to develop a high-security conservation park for endangered species, in their natural habitats, covering 100 square kilometres on the North East coast of KwaZulu-Natal, South Africa. The world's most technologically advanced conservation project ever undertaken, with a target build of £5 billion ($7 billion), it is scheduled to get underway in 2021.

The plan is enthusiastically supported by His Majesty, the King of the Zulus and leader of the region, Nkosi Tembe, under uMkhanyakude District.

The cost is major and yet this project, endorsed by government and conservation experts, has to be the start of many more to follow across the globe – if declining species are to be meaningfully returned to sustainable levels for tomorrow's generations. The price of inaction is unimaginable.

"The living biomass of terrestrial vertebrates on Earth today is represented by livestock 59%, human beings 36% and the sum of wild mammals, birds, reptiles and amphibians only 5%,"
frontiers in Conservation Science, Jan 2021

Figure 10 Anti-poaching rangers South Africa

Figure 11 Biodiversity crisis: Elephant in South Africa

Figure 12 Anti-poaching rangers South Africa

A New National PARK

"Major changes in the biosphere are directly linked to the growth of human systems... over 70% of the Earth's land surface has been altered by homo sapiens," *frontiers in Conservation Science, Jan 2021*

Figure 13 Wildlife area in South Africa, Noah's Ark on Afternoon Express (ZA)

The area will provide a safe, protected habitat for animals that includes a 20-30km^2 visitor and science compound. The park, Noah's Ark, will reconnect visitors of all ages with the diminishing animal kingdom and grow the support base of the 'everyman' concept; the idea is that each and every one of us has a role to play in safeguarding the balance of our eco systems.

The Visitor Centre will also embrace cutting-edge interpretative technology to educate adults and children about Noah's Ark's objectives and conservation impacts. As with the plans for the Natural History Museum in the adjacent leisure complex, the Centre will use interactive displays, multi-sensory activities and lifelike animal holograms to instil a sense of awe, wonder and respect for the natural world.

Figure 14 Biodiversity, Noah's Ark on Afternoon Express (ZA)

"More than two-thirds of the oceans have been compromised to some extent by human activities, live coral cover on reefs has halved in under 200 years,"
frontiers in Conservation Science, Jan 2021

"As of 2020, the overall material output of human endeavour exceeds the sum of all living biomass on Earth,"
frontiers in Conservation Science, Jan 2021

Figure 15 Biodiversity, Noah's Ark on Afternoon Express (ZA) (2 photos)

Figure 16 Lioness and cub (photo: Peta Photography)

"This rapid, catastrophic loss of biodiversity has reduced carbon sequestration and pollination, with further consequences of soil degradation, poorer water and air quality, more frequent and intense flooding and fires, and compromised human health,"
frontiers in Conservation Science, Jan 2021

The National Park includes:

Leading conservation technology

The project's innovative design, devised by DBM Architects South Africa, is underpinned by the primary objectives of protecting species on the endangered list and creating effective breeding programmes. The facility will also house world-class DNA and seed banks, making it possible for conservationists and ecologists to catalogue and share information on the fundamental blueprints of life. A laboratory complex linked to underground bunkers will provide secure storage for seeds and samples of animal DNA, offering a one-stop-shop to scientists in charge of managing and processing genetic material. Once the stuff of science-fiction fantasy, genetic engineering is opening up new possibilities, in targeting and replacing specific genomic sequences in living species closely related to extinct ones – in effect bringing back recently extinct specimens.

Leading scientists in strategic research

The complex will also enable leading scientists to undertake strategic research aimed at mitigating biological, predatory and poaching threats, for the purpose of removing animals from the endangered list. Working with a variety of global charitable projects, the Noah's Ark team will be a beacon of conservation excellence.

"UN Biodiversity targets agreed in Aichi Japan in 2010 acknowledged we have a responsibility to be stewards of the planet, because nature is important but also because people benefit directly from healthy, productive and resilient ecosystems and abundant biodiversity"
Science News 2020

Figure 17 Noah's Ark concept (photo: The Noah's Ark Foundation)

Figure 18 Noah's Ark concept (photo: The Noah's Ark Foundation)

"The air you breathe, the water you drink and the food you eat all rely on biodiversity, but right now it is in crisis – because of us.... scientists believe a sixth mass extinction has now begun or that current biodiversity losses mean we are heading in that direction."
The Guardian 2018

"Around 1 million species of plants and animals face extinction. We are eroding the very foundations of our economies, livelihoods, food security, health and quality of life worldwide"
U.N. Intergovernmental Science-Policy Platform on Biodiversity and Ecosystem Services 2019

"As the decade draws to a close many targets remain unmet. Currently, about 15% of land and 7.4% of seas are in some way protected, or in line for protection. Even so, current extinction rates are estimated to be 1,000 times higher than historical levels"
U.N. Environment Programme World Conservation Monitoring Centre

Figure 19 Biodiversity, Noah's Ark on Afternoon Express (ZA) (2 photos)

Figure 20 Biodiversity (2 photos: Peta Photography)

"The world has failed to meet a single target to stem the destruction of wildlife and life-sustaining ecosystems in the last decade"
UN on the state of nature 2020

Climate specific GeoDomes

Fifteen GeoDomes replicating the climates of environments across the planet, will include three large domes measuring 230m in diameter and 90m high, or as tall as a 30-storey building, occupying a space roughly three quarters of the size of Johannesburg's Sandton City shopping mall. These will replicate tropical, temperate and polar climates. Twelve sub-domes will replicate climates ranging from desert to Mediterranean, subarctic and highland. Each dome will be fitted with sophisticated smart glass technology for controlling the normal day/night cycles of the animals' natural habitats.

Figure 21 Noah's Ark GeoDomes & Aquarium (photo: The Noah's Ark Foundation)

"Natural World Heritage sites are under increasing pressure from climate change, infrastructure development, mining, poaching and other threats."
IUCN, official advisory body on nature under the World Heritage Convention.

The world's biggest aquarium

Water piped directly from the nearby Indian Ocean will create a life support system for the marine environment reproduced in the aquarium. The giant underwater observatory will provide conservationists with crucial data and allow visitors to enjoy magnificent sea life in its natural habitat.

"Climate change is now the biggest threat to natural World Heritage... and impacts from invasive alien species, such as house mice, Argentine ants and rainbow trout, may be greater than previously assessed."
IUCN, official advisory body on nature under the World Heritage Convention.

Figure 22 Noah's Ark Aquarium (photo: The Noah's Ark Foundation)

Community investment programme

As much as £500m will be invested in communities which rely on animal poaching to survive. The money will be used to create job opportunities and upgrade public services and infrastructure, such as hospitals, schools, roads and sanitation facilities. The fund will also pay for new social housing aimed at vastly improving local living conditions. Two communities, both of them heavily reliant on animal poaching as a source of income, have already been identified as key targets for support. The goal here is to restore a sense of pride among local people, introducing exciting opportunities for employment and nurturing greater responsibility for the environment in which the community lives and works.

Figure 23 Community & Leaders with the Noah's Ark team, in Noah's Ark location, KwaZulu-Natal ZA (2 photos)

Figure 24 Community & Leaders in Noah's Ark location, KwaZulu-Natal ZA (4 photos)

"Nature is crashing due to human activities. We need to respond as a global community and take personal responsibility in how we consume, vote and live. And we must push governments to take meaningful action."
U.N. Intergovernmental Science-Policy Platform on Biodiversity and Ecosystem Services 2019

In truth "Stopping biodiversity loss is nowhere close to the top of any country's priorities, trailing far behind other concerns such as employment, healthcare, economic growth, or currency stability,"
frontiers in Conservation Science, Jan 2021

Figure 25 Noah's Ark Team on location in KwaZulu-Natal ZA

Figure 26 Noah's Ark (photo: The Noah's Ark Foundation)

There is an answer. "The quarter of Earth's land now owned, used or occupied by indigenous communities holds about 80% of Earth's biodiversity. So empowering these groups to manage their lands could help countries achieve their targets."
Science News 2020,
World Bank report 2008

Making conservation strong and sustainable, with leisure

Our purpose is to engage, educate and build relationships with a new generation of environmental ambassadors. That includes reaching out to families, schools, researchers and experts; all of whom will need accommodation and leisure facilities when they visit the park. And, while tourism is not a primary objective for this charitable Foundation, such opportunities must be opened up for making conservation sustainable there.

The architectural scheme includes three hotels, for visitors to stay and experience the vital work that Noah's Ark's science and conservation teams will be undertaking. In addition, the leisure complex will include the following key features:

GeoDomes	*Entertainment Area*
Greenhouse	*Water Park Food Court*
Natural History Museum	*Bush Spa*
Conference Centre	*Hot Pools*

Appreciating how precious life is

"In the biblical story Noah is assured that, after building the Ark, God will never again send a global flood. As a sign of this promise, God points to a rainbow.

Our rainbow, our commitment to saving the planet's diverse species from extinction must be painted from a different palette. It must come from appreciating how precious life is, in all its forms and from every corner of the Earth; an appreciation which compels us to act before it's too late." – *Amy Stevens (Gifted Philanthropy)*

Amy Stevens is most definitely correct in saying that our rainbow should be painted from a different palette. Thus far we have only seen promises from world leaders in world summits, with new laws and regulations imposed on us as a population, but what exactly are the results? Some regard the latest Climate Change Summit with the theme "Climate Action Summit 2019: A Race We Can Win. A Race We Must Win." as an empty promise.

Figure 27 Noah's Ark concept (photo: The Noah's Ark Foundation)

MEDIA AND ENTERTAINMENT

Ark4Africa Music

Chris Avant Smith, Ark4Africa Concerts Executive Producer –

We are becoming more aware with every passing day that our planet is dying.

Helping to raise awareness and raise funds to combat the planet dying is Ark4Africa, the music arm of non-profit conservation gurus The Noah's Ark Foundation. Ark4Africa is currently working, in collaboration with Sony/ATV Music Publishing and Next Music, on the production of a Super Concert – with conservation the main theme – to be performed live in 2022.

Meanwhile, Ark4Africa has already released three songs with a conservation theme:

It's Just A Memory	It Takes the World to Make A Miracle	Blood On Our Hands
A song about the speed at which animals are being exterminated	A song on saving the planet with the Noah's Ark project	
Music arrangement:	Neill Solomon and Gary Judd (contribution)	Neill Solomon and Robin Hogarth
Composer: Neill Solomon and Gary Judd (contribution)	Neill Solomon	Robin Hogarth
Lyrics: Nicholas Ellenbogen	Neill Solomon	Robin Hogarth
Video concept & visualisation:	Andrew Timm	
Studio: Passage One Music	Passage One Music	Passage One Music
Vocals: Phathiswa Magangane	Phathiswa Magangane and Christina Mkabela	Phathiswa Magangane and Christina Mkabela
Remix produced by:	Dillon Barnard (DILL8N)	

For all three songs –
Producer: Neill Solomon and Robin Hogarth
Digital distribution: Next Music
Publishing: Sony Music Publishing
Executive producer: Dave Penhale (Sony Music Publishing)
Available to **BUY** from: music platforms worldwide

Robin Hogarth is a Double-Grammy® Award winner
Neill Solomon is highly acclaimed
Phathiswa Magangane appeared on The Voice South Africa
Gary Judd is a British film and television composer, from The Artful Corporation Ltd
Andrew Timm's creative credentials include his involvement in X Factor South Africa, Joyous Celebration, the SAFTA Awards, the Metro FM Awards, and countless other TV shows and live events over the past three decades. Andrew also directed the audition video for the Ndlovu Youth Choir which recently made it to the finals of America's Got Talent and a music video for Rustenburg High School of Queen's *Bohemian Rhapsody* which recently went viral on social media achieving two million views.

Figure 28 Song: It Takes the World to Make a Miracle (Ark4Africa) (2 photos)

25

It's Just A Memory

With the silence of a ghost
You tread the dusty earth
A giant from forgotten times
You have always been at hand
To share your strength and courage
With those weaker than yourself

I have drunk at wells you've made
In the dry of the river sand
And thought on and on
At the wonders of a land
That can desert you now
Let you die in some shadow place
Your rumble to become
Just a memory

Just a memory
Another time, another place
Just a memory
The shadow of wide wings
Drift across white sands
Tearing will begin
To return you to the land
Dust to dust

Just a memory
Another time, another place
Just a memory

It Takes the World to Make A Miracle

Intro
Wake Up, Wake Up, Why?
Wake Up, Wake Up, Wake Up,
Why? Why? Why?
Wake Up, Wake Up, Why?

Verse 1 & 2
No time left, no time left
Stop burying our heads in the sand
They came off the ark two by two
And found our blood thirsty hands
In the spirit land

Chorus 1
It takes the world to make a miracle
Without us it can't be done
Show your mettle, let's fight this war
Wake up or we'll be done
Wake up or we'll be gone
Wake up, wake up

Verse 3 & 4
In the sky, or underground
On the land, or underwater
Young and old, we're not alone
We better be looking after the spirit land

Bridge
We're living in a silent crisis
What's going to happen next?
We better get moving, do something fast
Or the planet's going to be laid to rest

We're living in a silent crisis
Watching the world go by
We don't realise, the planet's dying
And we're gonna have nowhere to hide

Chorus 1
It takes the world to make a miracle
Without us it can't be done
Show your mettle, let's fight this war
Wake up or we'll be done
Wake up or we'll be gone

Chorus 2
It takes the world to make a miracle
What's gonna happen next
We don't realise the planet's dying
And we're gonna have nowhere to hide

Chorus 3
It takes the world to make a miracle
It takes us all to be one
Love all creatures, create an ark
We are Noah, we are one
We are Noah, every one

Blood On Our Hands

Woza
So look around you
What do you see?
The earth is scorched
No man is free

Every day
The words don't rhyme
Forever lost
In endless time

Everywhere
The rhino dies
And the elephant:
The eagle cries

Not for his mate,
But for us all –
Time has run out,
Extinction calls

Chorus
There's blood on our hands,
It drips into
The dry dry earth.
We need to make a stand,
Instead of death, a new rebirth.
The land is crying,
Too much dying,
Time to make –
A stand

We're going to build,
Build an ark
A miracle
To light the dark

It takes the world
To make a change,
To take the spark
And light the flame

Chorus
There's blood on our hands,
It drips into
The dry dry earth.
We need to make a stand,
Instead of death, a new rebirth.
The land is crying,
Too much dying,
Time to make –
A stand

Phakama ! (rise up)

Figure 29 Song: It Takes the World to Make a Miracle (Ark4Africa)

Founder Richard says "We understand that times are hard at the moment for everyone, especially charities and conservation projects are no different. But everyone can do their bit to protect the environment and the animals with whom we share this planet. Recycling is one of the easiest and most important ways of protecting our wildlife. Plastic is a huge problem, not just in the oceans but also in the rainforests, arctic wilderness and our African plains.

People can get involved in so many different ways. We'd love people to play, download and stream these songs. And to be part of the resolve, interact with the hashtag #youarenoah. These are brilliant tracks and we're so proud to have released them to the world!"

In recent years, Sir David Attenborough has travelled from our screens to the Glastonbury main stage, Extinction Rebellion have ground cities to a halt and Greta Thunberg has shouted from the rooftops time and time again. We are taking more notice of recycling, and prioritising sustainable travel, but time is against us and we are in desperate need of a world-saving solution.

Of course, Extinction Rebellion and Greta alike have got our attention, but many are becoming tired of the action without any real action – and this includes Richard & Hein Prinsloo Curson. Taking action, over the last two years, the British-South African partners have put in motion their project to save animals from extinction and to preserve and improve the world for generations to come.

Their ground-breaking Noah's Ark project is an action to the ecosystem crisis the planet faces and to provide a way for everyone everywhere to get involved and be part of the solution; they aim to inspire unity so humanity will work together as one to fight the eco war, protect the circle of life, and encourage governments around the world to rethink their relationship with the planet and the animals that exist within it.

The park's aquarium is set to be the biggest in the world to accommodate ocean life, whilst Eden project-like GeoDomes, built using smart glass and sophisticated climate control systems, will ensure animals from other continents can feel at home in their own ecosystems under the South African sun. The Polar Dome, which needs to replicate the Arctic Eco System, is one of the toughest challenges facing the research and development teams.

We all know the original story of Noah's Ark being in the water, but this will be an 'ark' on the land, where an example of all animals and plants on Earth will be preserved and conserved. The Noah's Ark Foundation, a non-profit organisation set up to manage the Ark, will work to support global projects which prevent deforestation, pollution, hunting and the poaching of wild animals.

Noah's Ark TV Series 1

I know what you are thinking. Right? With all the hard work to get a £5 billion ($7 billion) project off the ground, namely Noah's Ark, why embark on a long TV Series – consisting of 13 seasons, with 12 episodes per season, starting early in 2021?

Well, the short answer is for global support. The four main aims of Noah's Ark are, to:

- Rescue and transfer animals with their habitats to the Ark, some to GeoDomes
- Incorporate designs at the very forefront of technology for wildlife protection
- Create a world-class centre of excellence in conservation supported by eco-tourism
- Bring about a worldwide change in culture in favour of environmental conservation

That's a very tall order in a world of warring governments and religions. In young sovereign states, struggling to catch up let alone deal with humanitarian issues, there is some public support for taking on climate change but practically none for wildlife conservation. Yet, inaction risks the very mass extinction feared by scientists.

That is why Noah's Ark aims to be a strong leader in conservation. And what it will take is culture change, right across the planet and at all levels of society from politicians and corporations to teachers, clergy and everyday people. All have a role, a vital one, in realising we humans "have a responsibility as stewards of the planet, because nature and the biosphere are important". The COVID-19 pandemic is our reality check as a global threat. The threat to nature is far greater.

That's where the TV series comes in. When we first started planning how the project might materialise, we would never have predicted the series would become such a big part. But, in reality, there is no greater medium than television to win over minds, young and old, and attract support and funding on this scale. That the series also showcases some misconceptions, about South Africa, is a bonus.

There is a fun side. When you watch a reality TV series, you often already know what to expect. But this series is different, as it follows the team on their journey to make the Ark a reality. It is unique in the sense that this has never been done – or even attempted – before. And, for that reason, the team is bound to encounter major challenges, losses and wins, which makes for great television.

Television is a great aid in educating on the importance of conservation

For our purposes, television is a great aid in educating youngsters on the importance of conservation. They are the future after all. The more we invest in them, the better it will be for people and the planet. A recent survey conducted in the UK, regarding children, television, and living green, gave these surprising results:

- 41% of children gained their knowledge from TV. This is better than expected, but come to think of it, with all the technology available to youngsters these days, it should not really be a surprise.
- Incredibly, 69% of parents have had a talking to by their kids on their environmental habits.
- Nine out of 10 parents said that their kids have a good understanding of the environment.

It does bear asking, whether parents listen to their children. Also, whether parents or kids are aware of the consequences of us abusing the environment.

Nonetheless, those school systems must be doing something right and, with a little more effort from us all, we could do even better across the world.

Figure 30 Richard & Hein with lion, at the Waterberg Predator Park, Vaalwater

NOAH'S ARK

Factual programming, education and entertainment

The Noah's Ark TV series aims to be a blend of factual programming, education and entertainment. Providing enjoyment for viewers while informing on what is happening to our environment – notably how we humans are dealing with issues, what we can change and how we can deal with environmental issues going forward. It is truly up to us to make a difference. #youarenoah

The programme, consisting of thirteen 12-episodes seasons, started on 18 January 2021 and this is a glimpse of the first four episodes.

It takes the world to make a miracle

Episodes open with wildlife across the planet, accompanied by the song *It takes the world to make a miracle* along with this voice over: *Consequences of what we do today will be felt by tomorrow's generation.*

Figure 31 Song: It Takes the World to Make a Miracle (Ark4Africa) (2 photos)

Figure 32 Plastic Pollution, Noah's Ark on Afternoon Express ZA

The world is dying for the second time in our history – we need to build an Ark. We must unite as one human species and save our planet. This is the greatest challenge we've ever faced; now it's time to take a stand as one single human race and build the 21st-century Noah's Ark.

Episode 1:
The team, predators & elephants

The park is described as consisting of an outer part, where animals have space to roam freely, an inner part with highly innovative climate-controlled GeoDomes and scientific laboratories, and a resort section that, very essentially, is to sustain the £5–10 billion pound ($7–14 billion) project.

Hosting most memorable celebrity parties

Co-founders Richard and Hein Prinsloo Curson introduce themselves. As a publicist Richard became a familiar face on the London social circuit hosting some of the most memorable celebrity parties in the capital, including a series of Club4Climate parties for climate change awareness. He also worked with the most famous media brands in the country including *OK!* Magazine and ITV. He has also worked with familiar faces and brands around the world, managing their impacts and impressions in the media. He has assisted in sharing news and views, working with media brands on special assignments, and helping to produce content for audiences around the world.

Richard tells how that background in publicity inspired him to do something truly worthwhile for the planet. Hein likewise was keen to put his experience in retail operations to work for the planet. Soon after

they found they shared that passion, in effect leaving a legacy for future generations, which is how the project started.

Now Richard is hard at work with so much to do and so little time to waste in each and every aspect of Noah's Ark, including production of the TV series and taking viewers on the journey to build a modern day, 21st-century Ark.

He and Hein emphasise the challenges ahead – such as the huge publicity needed in fundraising, engaging with leading conservationists and rescue centres for species they want to relocate there as well as planning and developing the Ark's designs and technologically advanced security systems.

The couple knew they couldn't do it alone, so they assembled a team that was to become the Noah's Ark family. All of whom appeared – Brett Rory Lipman Brand Manager, Christina Mkhabela Woman's Ambassador and Project Leader, Thobekile Ndlovu Noah's Ark Director for KZN, Omee Otis Ambassador, Polica Kgaugelo Sekhwela Community Director, Peta Janice Smith Animal Expert, Hannatjie Prinsloo Office and Team Manager. They introduce themselves and their roles in the project as well as the importance to them personally and the challenges ahead.

Figure 33 Richard Curson with celebrities in London

Figure 34 Noah's Ark team meeting on trip to KZN

The first steps are fundraising and leasing the land where they would like to build Noah's Ark. Thobe reveals in a call that she has nailed down a meeting with Chief Tembe, ruler of the Tembe Traditional Council, and the team meets to discuss the Tembe land. She advises that the Zulu are very traditional people, with strict protocols and signs of respect that need to be adhered to in meeting them – such as taking a gift. Omee is a little upset, in their discussing arrangements to travel to Ballito and then to the Chief and his council, as he is left out. He takes it well though.

Peta then takes us to a couple of rescue and rehabilitation sanctuaries the Ark is working with, in South Africa. First is the Waterberg Predator Park, Vaalwater, where she introduces us to rescue wolves and wild cats. There are beautiful shots of her getting close with a wolf and then a lion.

Next is Adventures with Elephants, in Bela Bela, Limpopo, where owner Sean Hensman shares his conservation, research and education project with us. In which he raises awareness about land that is being taken, with humans overpopulating, and how elephants are then confined to areas of the worst quality.

Peta introduces his elephant friends as ecosystem engineers and joins Sean up close to a group, in describing them in great detail.

The episode ends with the team getting ready to travel, with a little frustration as Kgaugelo is late, and then they set off to Ballito, KwaZulu-Natal (KZN).

Figure 35 Peta with wolf, at Waterberg Predator Park

Figure 36 Peta with lion, at Waterberg
Predator Park

Figure 37 Sean Hensman at Adventures with Elephants

Figure 38 Peta at Adventures with Elephants

Episode 2: Anti-poaching & preparing to meet the Chief

The team hit the road from Johannesburg to Durban. We follow on their adventure to the coast, getting to know them a little more as their personalities begin to reveal themselves. Travelling with people will always reveal your pet peeves and character quirks.

Along the way we see some of the beautiful countryside that is South Africa as they drive through the mountain passes and midlands that take us to our destination. KwaZulu-Natal (KZN) is also known as the Garden Province with its lush tropical greenery, breath-taking mountain ranges, beautiful beaches, diverse culture and modern sophistication.

The team arrives in Durban, checks into their accommodation, and spends the rest of the afternoon relaxing on the beautiful beaches of Ballito. The day ends with a team dinner where they toast to the first potential success of their journey.

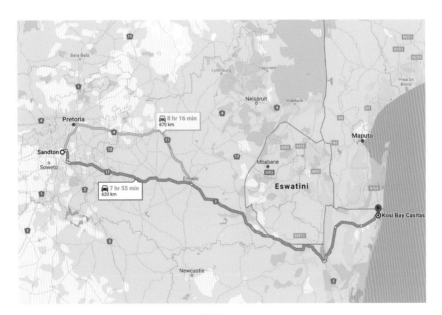

Figure 39 Map: route from Joburg to KZN

Figure 40 The countryside in KZN

Figure 41 The seaside in KZN

Thobe informs Richard and Hein that they need to go shopping for a gift for the Chief; they can't go empty handed. The next day, Richard and Hein hit the stores to find the perfect gift for the Chief.

While the boys shop up a storm in Ballito, back in Limpopo it's a big change of scene for Ark team member Omee Otis, who is known for his music.

But now he feels a bit like a fish out of water as he's transplanted to the African bush. One of the biggest issues for wildlife conservation is poaching. The illegal trade in animal parts has become an incredibly big business in South Africa.

Dedicated to keeping SA's 'Big 5' safe

But there is a fight back. Arthur Crew heads up the HRU anti-poaching unit, posted mostly at local wildlife conservation projects in Limpopo and Gauteng. They are dedicated to keeping South Africa's 'Big 5' safe from the cruel killing of poachers and from extinction.

Figure 42 Buying a gift for Chief Tembe

Figure 43 Omee singing

Anti-poaching combat training

Arthur prepares to give Omee a crash course in anti-poaching combat training. He starts with introducing the problem, specifically around rhino, lion, tiger, leopard and whatever else. Omee is clearly excited but, on being introduced to the bullet proof vests they wear, he's disappointed on hearing he is not mean enough to take on some of the criminals they have to deal with.

The conservation project they're in is home to a very successful breeding and safety programme for some of Africa's big cats. Omee meets some of these kitties and is taken aback: "Boom, comes this huge baby. I probably thought this is one of the biggest lions in the jungle but then hey they tell me it's probably like eight months old."

Figure 44 A rhino mother killed by poachers

Figure 45 Poaching of rhino horns

Figure 46 Omee meets a kittie, actually a lion

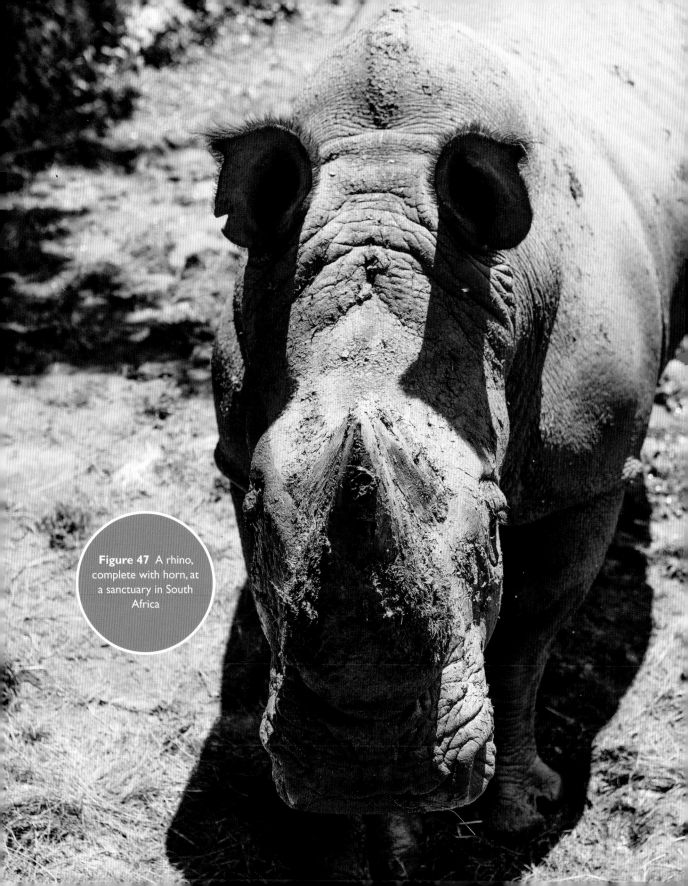

Figure 47 A rhino, complete with horn, at a sanctuary in South Africa

In the media, Arthur explains, it's largely been about poaching rhino for their horns which are sold around the world. "Muti, that kind of thing." Muti is sold as a 'medicine' in Africa to empower and heel people, while rhino horn is also sold elsewhere as an aphrodisiac. Scientific studies have shown these to be myths, rhino horn has neither of those properties. The heads of big cats are sold worldwide as trophies.

Arthur takes Omee off to the firing range to see how or if this little package of dynamite handles a big gun. "That gun is as big as you." Bam, Omee shoots and is shocked at the kick-back, "Phew I don't think I was ready for that."

Back in KZN, Umhlanga is an affluent residential, commercial and resort town on the coast north of Durban, where Richard, Hein and team are invited to lunch at Thobe's home.

The meal is phenomenal and they are able to pick her brain before meeting the chief the next day. Dress code, not to offend she explains, is as important as the right greeting.

Meanwhile, the HRU is called out to a snare, giving Omee a chance to see a real situation play out and ask a lot more questions.

At sunrise the next day, the team climbs into the car with butterflies in their tummies, today is a big day and the stakes are high. If the Chief refuses to give them the land they need, to build Noah's Ark, they will be back to the drawing board.

The second part of this road trip begins. Hein is at the wheel as they head out into the most rural parts of the KwaZulu-Natal coastline. After five hours of driving the team finally arrive at their destination.

Figure 48 Poaching, Noah's Ark s1 ep 1

Figure 49 Poaching, Noah's Ark s1 ep 1

Figure 50 Preparing with Thobe to meet the chief

Figure 51 Omee with anti-poaching rangers

Figure 52 Community hardship in KZN

Figure 53 Thobe in a market in KZN

The opportunity to earn decent incomes

Richard reflects on having seen on the journey how the locals are less fortunate, less wealthy, "It just breaks my heart every time I see how people in South Africa live. It just brings home why Noah's Ark is so important here. It's going to give these people the opportunity to earn decent incomes and build decent houses."

The team take a little detour on their way to meet the Chief and stop off at a roadside market that holds many treasures. The little stalls can be found throughout South Africa along the main highways and roads that connect cities and towns. The beadwork is a big part of Zulu culture, bead colours hold different meanings and family names are often associated with powerful animals like elephants, bulls, lions or crocodiles. Selling such produce puts food on their tables.

Thinking they are heading straight to the proposed site for Noah's Ark, the team are instead thrown a curveball and forced to diverge from their course. Expecting to have a one on one with Chief Tembe on the land itself, they find out they are first expected to pitch Noah's Ark to the Chief and his council before being given permission to view the land. Not expecting that, they rock up in shorts and not at all the right dress code.

The presentation goes ahead nevertheless and Chief Tembe and his council ask Richard and Hein to pay a deposit of seed funding for the land. Also, the Chief would like to see the team get involved with his community. Finally, Richard found a moment, albeit a little awkwardly barging in on the Chief, to give him their gifts.

The proposal was accepted in principle

Another hour's drive away, on a rough road where they get stuck and have to hitch a lift on a pick-up (bakkie in South Africa), they finally reach the land everyone has been talking about. This is truly one of the most breath-taking parts of South Africa. The land is untouched, well preserved and valued by the Chief and his people. Though the proposal was accepted in principle by the Chief, the team still have a lot of work to make sure this project, and the land, actually happen. The dream is yet to come to life.

Figure 54 Richard presents to the Chief & his Council

Episode 3: A Royal Meeting

The team are now standing on Noah's Ark land, on the soil, or at least where they want for the Ark. Richard expresses that the smell, such a magical smell of nature, is an indescribable smell actually of sweets flowers. A beautiful smell. One hundred square kilometres of beautiful sunsets, lush wilderness and a future home to the planet's animals.

Team member Peta Janice Smith says it's wonderful, there's no words to describe it. And the best part is she's spotted some signs of wildlife. Small wildlife, a mouse, but still it's wildlife. Hein sees them utilising the river for the restaurant and waterfall, maybe the train coming from the opposite side. Richard chips in where he sees the domes. The land may not look like much now but it will be a lifeline to not only animals but also the people in the region.

Figure 55 Hein & Richard view the land for NA

Dire need to help women in the community

The team waste no time in bringing in community expert Christina Mkhabela, to start working with the community, getting to know what they need, and getting the word out about Noah's Ark. They call a meeting to catch up with what's going on, that Peta had left for Joburg to see the monkey sanctuary and Christina had come in. Since arriving they could see a dire need to help women in the community. They aim to paint the hall, while Christina meets with the community.

Figure 56 Richard, Hein, Thobe & Kgaugelo

Habitats destroyed by building cities

Peta is meanwhile at the Bambelela Wildlife Care & Vervet Monkey Rehabilitation Farm, in Bela Bela. Though Bambelela works with all its wildlife, it's most regarded for its exceptional work with vervet monkeys. Peta meets with tour guide Nicky Jones, and explains monkeys come there mainly due to human negligence or because their habitats have been destroyed by building cities. The project takes them in, rehabilitates them and then sends them back into the wild where they have a second shot at life.

Figure 57 Peta with Vervet Monkeys

gure 58 (above) Peta & guide Nicky with Vervet Monkeys, (below) chard, Hein & Thobe help the Tembe Community

39

The team, meanwhile, go to the community hall and find more than painting is needed. The centre has broken windows, doors falling off, and the roof is leaking. They resolve to do something each time they visit. For now it's painting and they head for the hardware store.

Figure 59 Hein, Richard, Kgaugelo Community work

Then they run into a snag. Thobe arrives, saying the Chief would like the outside painted, when the paint bought is for the inside. She reassures them, being in construction this is her space, the paint bought is OK for the task. Then team member Polica Kgaugelo Sekhwela brings in some local experts to help out with painting.

Spreading the word about Noah's Ark

Joining in with the community is a good way of spreading the word about Noah's Ark. It's the perfect project for creating jobs to break the cycle of poverty stemming back to the apartheid era.

Christina finally returns with news of a widow in desperate need of help. Her husband just passed away, the main provider of the family, and then some local thugs took advantage and burnt down her house. The family lost everything. The team decide to drop everything, Kgaugelo and Christina taking Richard and Hein to see where she and her three children are living is made of mud and sticks. It leaks and there is no protection from snakes. What they are eating has no nutrients, the space is cramped and it's smoky. They resolve to make a plan to help her, once they are back in Joburg. Noah's Ark is not just about saving animals, they care about the community and won't stand by and do nothing.

Noah's Ark's ultimate mission, releasing animals safely to the wild

Back in Bambelela, Peta is now with monkeys in the final stage of rehabilitation. This is where they come before being released, and then be completely wild monkeys. That is Noah's Ark's ultimate mission,

Figure 60 Christina & Kgaugelo help a stricken lady

releasing animals safely to the wild. Some are never released and live their days out in the sanctuary. One such was injured in the mouth and blinded, when some youngsters thought it fantastic over New Year to put a firecracker inside a banana.

At the community hall, they'd managed to finish painting the entire exterior of the building. Though a small thing, the team are encouraged in thinking the Chief will be pleased. And to show their appreciation, the community treats the Noah's Ark team to experience traditional Zulu dancing. A big Zulu tradition, with vibrant singing and beating of drums. Historically, young warriors would build up their courage before a battle with the mesmerising Zulu drums. Richard is so excited he even joins in, though looking a little ridiculous, with not getting the moves right yet. Thobe also joins. In all, it goes down well though.

Figure 61 Traditional Zulu dance, Chief & Richard

Episode 4: Good Morning Britain

The team continues its journey in KZN and, searching for another local community in need, they decide to go to the Manzengwenya primary school. They meet the children and soon discover the school is too rural for the government to administer the proper aid. And, with poverty being high, there is little that can be done by the community. The school lacks proper desks and chairs as well as sanitation, playgrounds are dilapidated and they don't have enough teachers.

Providing jobs and better schooling

"It's an amazing experience arriving at the school, with those little ones so happy to see us. So hungry or so excited, we literally felt like celebrities and just to see those big smiles it was great to be there." Once Noah's Ark is built all of that would change, in terms of providing jobs and better schooling.

Richard, finding a piece of wood lying about, decides to have a bit of fun and teach the kids how to play a game of rounders. Christina joins in, and Thobe soon gets the hang of it. It's all in the spirit that Noah's Ark is not all about animals but also communities and working together to preserve life for future generations.

Peta is busy at a vulture sanctuary and rehabilitation centre, Vulpro, hearing from Kerry Volter there about its beginnings in 2007 with a handful of birds and

Figure 62 Christina with school children

Figure 63 Richard plays rounders with school children

Figure 64 Richard, Thobe & Kgaugelo give presents to school children

Figure 65 Capturing Vultures to be released

Figure 66 Vultures fly free

Figure 67 Peta with Kerry at the release site

Figure 68 Peta & others release the Vultures

how it's grown. Most of the birds are from power line collisions and electrocutions, and few of those can ever be released. There are 22 to 23 species that can be found on all continents except for Australia and Antarctica. In the past 15 years there's been a 90% decline, putting many species on a critically endangered list.

Vultures play a vital role in nature

Vultures play a vital role in nature, by cleaning carcasses quickly. Without that clean up, infectious diseases are apt to sit in the environment and pass on to other species. Nature has those fine balances in the ecosystem; every creature big or small has its role to play. The more species we lose, the more unstable it will all become.

In December, 18 young birds came in for rehabilitation and they're all good to go now. The

centre prepares to give them their freedom, which begins by catching them – not an easy task – and then crating them for transfer by truck.

In Joburg, Richard receives incredible news from Claire Barber PR in the UK. It's a truly great opportunity. Noah's Ark is going live on ITV's *Good Morning Britain*, in 48 hours. The anxiety and stress, but also an overall joy, is immediate.

Meanwhile Peta and the Vulpro team arrive at an escarpment, where they unload the crates. Stress levels in the crates are high. But they couldn't have picked a more spectacular spot to release these magnificent creatures back into the wild. They can actually feel the wind coming up, ideal for the vultures to launch into and effortlessly climb the thermals.

The crates are lined up and, on the count of three, two, one… the gates are lifted. Tenuously at first, they spread their wings and soar away.

Figure 69 One of the released Vultures soaring free

THE LATEST
MODERN-DAY NOAH'S ARK
£5 billion conservation project aims to preserve every plant and animal on planet

Figure 70 Adil Ray & Charlotte Hawkins, Modern-Day Noah's Ark on ITV's Good Morning Britain

Figure 71 Richard Curson with Sean Hensman at Adventures with Elephants, Modern-Day Noah's Ark on ITV's Good Morning Britain

ITV's Good Morning Britain, with Adil Ray and Charlotte Hawkins

In the UK, Noah's Ark goes live on ITV's *Good Morning Britain*, with Adil Ray and Charlotte Hawkins presenting. Charlotte: "On to something quite incredible. It is described as one of the most ambitious ecological schemes in history. But, preparations for a Noah's Ark-style conservation park to protect the animal kingdom are underway in South Africa."

Adil: "This futuristic park in KwaZulu-Natal province aims to preserve every species on the planet. We will be live in South Africa to talk to the people behind the vast project."

Figure 72 Noah's Ark on ITV's Good Morning Britain

Cameras show the crew behind the scenes, Adventures with Elephants director Sean Hensman is at their site with Richard. Tensions are high, failure would be dire. With over a million viewers this is the largest morning show in the UK.

Tom Barton, voiceover: "The animals in our world are not yet extinct but they could be. And this modern-day Noah's Ark aims to stop that from happening.

"This way the founders believe the animal kingdom now approaching crisis point can be saved for future generations. Protected from extinction, from the combined threats of climate change, hunters, poachers, and deforestation."

Figure 73 Richard with Sean Hensman on camera

Charlotte: "It is quite incredible. WWF reported in 2018 that humans have wiped out 60% of Earth's animals since 1970. How do you choose which animals you are going to have there, or are you literally going to have as many as possible?"

Richard hides his anxiety well in responding: "We'll focus on animals that are really facing extinction right now. That is our priority. But we do want to bring in as many adults as we can into the project, eventually all of them."

More questions raised by Adil and Charlotte are answered much the same as in Episode 1.

Charlotte: "We wish you the best of luck with it. It's a huge undertaking. If it succeeds it will be a very special thing for animal conservation." That ended an extremely good interview on *Good Morning Britain*.

Figure 74 Peta at Adventures with Elephants

Figure 75 Peta on ITV's Good Morning Britain

Figure 76 Richard with Sean Hensman, on camera at Adventures with Elephants

47

94.2
jacarandafm

JACARANDA FM
Company, Community or Culture?

South Africa's Biggest Commercial Radio Station

When Noah's Ark co-founder Richard Prinsloo Curson approached Jacaranda FM to help generate awareness for the most ambitious and impactful conservation project on the planet, the much-loved South African radio station jumped at the opportunity to feature the project.

Noah's Ark and Jacaranda FM resonate so wonderfully together

Jacaranda FM has periodically been involved in conservation efforts as part of their larger approach to community upliftment, but it was a deeper, 'community-first' ethos that saw Noah's Ark and Jacaranda FM resonate so wonderfully together.

Figure 77 Richard & Hein Prinsloo-Curson on air at Jacaranda FM talking about Noah's Ark

Community First

Jacaranda FM puts their community at the centre of everything they do. Their content is curated to inform locals with news relevant to their needs. Music is researched to reflect the community's taste, and events are centred around activities commonly shared by families.

Jacaranda FM has changed the lives of their community on a weekly basis

Perhaps the biggest feather in their cap is that Jacaranda FM is the only commercial radio station in South Africa that has changed the lives of their community on a weekly basis, for the past 16 years through Good Morning Angels.

Good Morning Angels, is a special weekly community upliftment feature on the Jacaranda FM morning show. Every Wednesday morning, with the assistance of donors and listeners, Good Morning Angels assists individuals, organisations, and communities with all manner of need. The idea is simple: Jacaranda FM invites people to send requests for help on behalf of people in need. Then, they try to find a sponsor who can help by leveraging their giant network and expertise. If they succeed, the station brings the sponsor and the recipient together and shares stories of inspiration with their community.

What makes the radio station so successful is that they are unlike most businesses. Jacaranda FM is not mandated to focus on specific Corporate Social Investment (CSI) initiatives, but rather directs assistance to where it is needed, as dictated by the community. This differentiator has ensured that the station is led by the need and not the usual red-tape, which in turn provides greater goodwill currency.

"When our community is happy, we lead the celebration. When our community is in need or crisis, we give a voice to those in need, do what we can to assist, and support or solve the problem. It's all about our listeners," says Deirdre King, Jacaranda FM Managing Director.

Curate the Currency of Goodwill

Never has the currency of goodwill (the true value of CSI for those who insist on balance sheets to prove return on investment) been more calculable, impactful, and tangible. Goodwill is how Jacaranda FM was able to raise R5 million for farmer aid in the Free State following the devastating fires in October 2020. "The economy was at its lowest point and still we managed to help. This is the power of goodwill and it yields impressive results. The paradox is, that in order to achieve these results, you cannot focus on them, you can only focus on the people or animals that need our help," adds King.

When it comes to helping individuals or communities, Jacaranda FM understands the value of goodwill - that invisible string that binds us, the attitude that no task is too small or big, and magic that happens when people rally together for a common cause without personal or professional gain. Goodwill has become the invisible brand-armour that builds loyalty and a positive brand reputation and resonance. It's what gives your business intangible value that cannot be replicated, and it's what consumers seek when trying to identify if your brand identity echoes theirs.

Figure 78 Jacaranda radio studio ZA

Echoing an Identity

Because the ambitions of Noah's Ark spoke so strongly to the community identity that Jacaranda FM values, the station gave Noah's Ark the opportunity to take-over their prime-time morning drive programme in January 2021.

Jacaranda FM gave Noah's Ark the opportunity to take over their prime-time morning drive programme in January 2021

By nature, radio is a one-on-one medium. Millions of people listen to their audio and digital devices at any given time, but radio speaks directly to the person listening. It's an intimate discussion between a trusted, familiar voice and a loyal listener.

In the mind of their listeners, the station and Noah's Ark show up as caring and involved. Listeners also take considerable pleasure and pride in 'doing their bit' by supporting a project the station shares with them. "We echo their identity or the part of themselves they want to be, and it's one of the contributing factors to our longevity and trust in the space," adds King.

Jacaranda FM has, through Good Morning Angels and other initiatives, proven to be the commercial radio station that not only cares, but acts and rallies others to do the same. Their audience is emotionally invested and connects with the brand on a very personal level; listeners don't only have the radio on, they listen, participate, trust, and support and it's this type of engagement that they were happy to offer in aid of Noah's Ark.

Figure 79 Hein Prinsloo Curson

In 2013 the station created an incredible telethon to raise over R300 000 for the 'Give Kili Horns' project as part of their Purple Rhino project. Jacaranda FM eventually raised over R1.5 million for rhino conservation in South Africa. In 2017 the station assisted Knysna by gifting them their own fire truck when the town was devastated by fire, and rebuilt Laerskool Protearif in Krugersdorp within three months after a tornado damaged the school in 2018.

From their efforts, it's clear to see the station cares deeply for the community, so much so that it's become a culture within the company.

Figure 80 Richard & Hein Prinsloo Curson

Beyond Community into a Culture

"Jacaranda FM has managed to create a culture of community responsibility. It's built into our weekly programming, attracts various sponsors, and because we've consistently served the community for the past 16 years; our listeners have come to depend on and expect Good Morning Angels to be there to fulfil whatever need may arise," adds King.

Jacaranda FM, a commercial radio station in Gauteng, South Africa has shown us that it is possible to transcend community and develop a culture where doing good, conservation, community upliftment,

natural disaster relief, and personal assistance become a regular part of what we do because we are listening to the community around us.

About Jacaranda FM

Jacaranda FM broadcasts at 94.2FM from Midrand, Gauteng and is one of most popular radio stations with the second-largest footprint across South Africa. The station has the only bilingual commercial licence in the country; broadcasting regionally in English and Afrikaans across Gauteng, Limpopo, Mpumalanga, and the North West Province.

Figure 81 Richard Prinsloo Curson

Afternoon Express

Interviewed by presenter Palesa Tembe on South Africa's popular Afternoon Express TV show (October 2020) Hein explained that what started off being for rhinos five years previously, ended up being a fully-fledged global conservation project. Richard went on to say how we in the human race have a responsibility for each other and the world that we live in. The Noah's Ark project is creating a platform where everyone in the world can take that responsibility, by getting involved, and be 'Noah' to save the planet.

Palesa was interested in the hashtag #youarenoah, to which Richard said it is a message in social media, for everyone in the world to join and take part. He added that they are making a TV series, for everyone to see what the project is doing in South Africa – working with South African people and businesses, to make this a reality, but also to empower local communities and step up efforts to irradicate poaching.

On the question posed by Palesa, on the park's sustainability, Richard expressed that Noah's Ark is a

Figure 82 Palesa Tembe on Afternoon Express ZA

celebration of South Africa as much as it is of animals and climate change issues. "We want to invite people from around the world to come and see it. Those visitors will help to keep it going as a legacy, long into the future."

Figure 83 Richard with Peta

Figure 84 Hein with Christina

Figure 85 Palesa Tembe with Richard & Hein, Afternoon Express ZA

RICHARD PRINSLOO-CURSON | @noahsarklife
President: The Noah's Ark Foundation

Figure 86 Richard on Afternoon Express ZA

HEIN PRINSLOO-CURSON | @noahsarklife
Vice-President: The Noah's Ark Foundation

Figure 87 Hein on Afternoon Express ZA

Figure 88
Noah's Ark
conception on
Afternoon
Express ZA

eNCA

Richard Prinsloo Curson was interviewed on eNCA TV South Africa by anchor Uveka Rangappa, on 28 February 2020, on how South Africa could become home to one of the most technologically advanced conservation parks. And how it would preserve every animal species in the world. Uveka put to him, "I'm sure many will be asking: are you crazy to try to tackle this? What's involved?"

Richard replied: "Many things. We've had to meet the support of communities, where we want to build the Ark. But also, we are reaching out to win support from every single person on the planet. We're doing that with a number of initiatives, including music and entertainment. We're making a television series to document the process and all the work involved. And that series is being broadcast around the world.

My favourite part of the park is the GeoDomes, as those are climate replications of areas not in Africa. We are working with technology companies to replicate other parts of the world, for instance the Arctic. The polar dome is the star of the show."

Figure 89 Richard with Uveka Rangappa on eNCA TV ZA

Figure 90 Richard introducing Noah's Ark conception on eNCA TV ZA

PLANNING

Relocation of Species and Habitats

So, as you can imagine, a Land Ark comes with its own big challenges which the team needs to face and resolve. It is no easy task building a 21st-century Ark. And, to be honest, we need all the help we can get to overcome the obstacles. Finding animals from all over the world and re-locating them to the Ark upon completion will be a massive enough task; just think of the planning and execution required to move a whale or even a polar bear to the Ark.

Global Invasive Species Programme (GISP) has the following summary of potential impacts: "Invasive non-native species can harm individual native species or even entire ecosystems, and thus also impact those who depend on natural systems for important resources and products. Unlike other kinds of pollution, these 'biological pollutants' can actually increase in abundance over time and force out native species – by competing with them (for space, water, or food), by eating the native species, spreading new diseases, or so altering the habitat that the native species can no longer survive. In fact, the impacts of non-native species are now recognised as second only to habitat alteration as a factor in the decline and extinction of our American flora and fauna."

This of course means the Noah's Ark Team has no idea of the challenges, but that there would be such. We now have to find the experts to develop the GeoDomes, in itself no easy task, but not impossible.

Figure 91 Endangered: Polar Bear

Polar Bears International have done a brilliant job explaining the collapse of polar bear populations, imparting relevant information to the Noah's Ark project. Elements in the design and development strategy for the GeoDome habitats need to be fully thought out.

Is it doable? We don't know, but Noah's Ark will get there. Development of the design is being undertaken by DBM Architects, Johannesburg, South Africa. They are renowned all around Africa for their innovative thinking and as a creative team that makes dreams a reality. When Noah's Ark first met with DBM, it was love at first sight. They immediately took the project on and totally transformed it from its beginning; it took a painstakingly long time, meeting after meeting, drawing after drawing, to get the designs to what they are now. But it is not over yet. What we have is a dream concept in drawings, a theoretical design, that the project needs to transform from paper to reality.

The design looks brilliant and one can see that DBM have put a lot of passion into the project, as they do with all projects they embark on. But will it turn out the way we want? There is no way of telling at this stage, as we need experts to guide us in what is realistic, practical and doable, with the technology currently available or in development. Technology that is cutting-edge and even pushing beyond.

Figure 92 Endangered: New Zealand Falcon

Figure 93 Endangered: Canadian Lynx

Figure 94 Endangered: Blue Sowthistle

Figure 95 Endangered: Bumblebee

Endangered Species:
African Wild Dog   Barbary Ape   Lemur

Figure 96 Noah's Ark concept: GeoDomes area

Endangered Species:
South African Crane   Red Panda   Green Turtle

Interdependence of Plants & Animals

Plants & Us

Noah's Ark features in a new book coming out this autumn. It is called *Plants & Us How they shaped human history and society*. It not only stresses the vital role of plants in our lives, but also looks at the importance of preserving animals as a way of preserving plants. Hence the link with the Noah's Ark project.

The chapter headings in the new book set the very varied themes: Plants as Heroes, Plants as Villains and above all, Plants in Peril. This covers the threat from humans, like deforestation and the growth of monocultures, to the devastating effects of climate change – wildfires, floods, desertification, salination and falls in water tables. As the writers point out, '*If the plants disappear, then the base of earth's ecosystems will go and with that, all present terrestrial life forms, including us*'.

But there is ample evidence that animals being under threat means that their habitats will be in trouble, such is the intimate relationship between plants and animals, insects, birds and fish. The absolutely vital pollination of plants and flowers by insects is one of the most powerful examples, but there are plenty of others.

Figure 97 The Eden Project Cornwall UK, aerial view (photo: The Eden Project)

It is not surprising that the Foreword of the book is written by Sir Tim Smit, the pioneer who created the Eden Project in England's Cornwall. Tim Smit was certainly no novice at creating drama. Trained as an anthropologist, he had made a career in the pop music world, as a songwriter and producer earning seven platinum and gold discs. So, he was more than familiar in putting on a show and pulling in the punters.

Having moved to Cornwall, he caught the public imagination by restoring the nearby Lost Gardens of Heligan and became fascinated by how to get people really interested in plants by weaving human stories around them – tales of adventure, emotion and derring-do. At Eden he thought that there was an even bigger story to be told; of the plants that shaped the world as we know it and of our total dependence on, and connection to, the natural environment.

His small team bought an exhausted, 160-year-old, steep-sided china clay quarry 60 metres deep, with no soil, and gave it life. There they planned a huge diversity of plants, planted into soil made from 'waste' materials, watered by the rain, in giant and awe-inspiring conservatories and buildings that drew inspiration from nature.

Just over 20 years later in a deep crater in Cornwall, two covered Biomes, nestle into a south-facing cliff face. The Tropical Biome houses the largest rainforest 'in captivity', with banana plants, coffee, rubber and bamboos. The Mediterranean Biome, its little sister, features warm temperate plants like olives and grape vines, while the scimitar-shaped Outdoor Gardens display temperate plants like tea, lavender, hops, hemp and sunflowers.

The 15-hectare Eden site has proved to be a valuable focus and shop window for public and media interest in plants. Every year it attracts over a million visitors of all ages and interests, with a further two and a half million to its website. It has had a huge positive impact on tourism in the county and is an important driver in the local economy, estimated to have injected two billion pounds (2.75 billion US dollars) into Cornwall's economy.

Figure 98 Photo: The Eden Project, rain forest

Figure 99 Sir Tim Smit, The Eden Project Founder

Plants & Us features several 'glasshouses' that have transformed the way we can look at plants indoors, from Joseph Paxton's 'Great Conservatory' at Chatsworth and the Crystal Palace, to Missouri Botanic Garden's 'Climatron'. The two modern huge domes at The Eden Project are great precursors for the many GeoDomes of Noah's Ark.

Even as the conservation movement expanded from the 1960s, plants were for a long time overlooked by both the general public and the conservation establishment. Animals make great TV stars and, not only do plants compare badly with birds and small furry mammals in their emotional appeal, but also the plant kingdom at first sight lacks 'big cuddlies' – the bears, elephants, lions, tigers, leopards and other cats, and the much-loved giant panda.

Plants are central to life on Earth

This is unfortunate because plants are absolutely central to life on Earth. They derive their energy and ability to survive, grow and reproduce from the harvest of sunlight; hence they are the primary source of all the energy in the food chains that enable animals and humans to exist and survive. They absorb and fix carbon dioxide in the presence of sunlight and the green plant pigment chlorophyll, using the sun's energy to split water molecules and convert carbon into sugars and other plant foods, while releasing oxygen, on which life depends.

Then there is vegetation – the complex communities that plants form – which is the structural basis of most of the ecological systems which animals and humans inhabit. Animals eat plants and live and nest among them. Plants maintain the physical and chemical integrity of these complex natural and modified 'ecosystems' by providing a range of vital ecological 'goods and services'. *En masse* they trap the water vapour of mist, fog and clouds, they moderate wind, rain and water run-off, their roots consolidate unstable slopes, gravel, mud and blown sand and their dead remains build up soils.

It is to be hoped that pioneering initiatives like Noah's Ark and The Eden Project will focus the world on how animals and plants have an intimate relationship – and that both must be preserved.

Building the World's Largest Aquarium

Among the biggest challenges, if not the biggest, will be designing, building and filling the sea aquarium. Each stage demands unrivalled expertise, from researching and selecting species complete with their habitats, to building and testing the structures, and finally populating them and keeping the inhabitants safe and well – and, most crucially, wild. What is inescapable, is that none of that effort can ever end.

The planet is largely covered by oceans (close to 71%) a great deal of which is unmapped. And 94% of life on Earth is in those depths, according to the USA Science & Engineering Festival.

"More than 80% of the ocean remains unexplored": Oceana 8 June 2020 and, in consequence, "only about 7% of the world's oceans are designated as marine protected areas (MPAs)… Oceana has protected nearly 4 million square miles of ocean to date." The real danger is that: "Scientists do not have a complete understanding of how one change to the ocean affects the entire ecosystem [or how all the pieces fit together] and which of those changes may be the tipping point that causes collapse."

"Around 700 ocean sites are now suffering from low oxygen, compared with 45 in the 1960s": Concluded the biggest study of its kind, undertaken by conservation group IUCN, BBC News 7 December 2019.

And "50–80% of the oxygen production on Earth comes from the ocean.": National Ocean Service, National Oceanic and Atmospheric Services, US Department of Commerce.

The aquarium and research facilities are high priority

In short, indications are the planet's air system is overloaded, with demands from us that are rising out of control. As it stands, without fully comprehending how nature works and especially in the oceans, system breakdown is a certainty. We are demanding more than the planet's capacity to deliver, even before factoring in the current explosion in populations and disposable incomes.

The aquarium and research facilities are high priority for Noah's Ark – expressly so that, in association with other conservation interests worldwide, ocean biodiversity can be explored, studied and protected before it's too late.

Figure 100 Endangered species: African Penguin

Figure 101 Endangered species: Sea Otter

Figure 102 IUCN Red List: Galapagos Penguin

Figure 103 (above) The Noah's Ark Aquarium is to be the largest in the world (below) IUCN endangered red list: Manta Ray, Florida Manatee

Figure 104
IUCN endangered red list: Blue Whale

Figure 105
IUCN
endangered
red list: Whale
Shark

International Union for Conservation of Nature (IUCN) Red List of Endangered Species Dec 2020

There are now 128,918 species on the IUCN Red List, of which 35,765 are threatened with extinction. Among which: The giant manta ray is at a very high risk of extinction and four hammerhead shark species are

TV series Tanked, for his and Anthony Mark Carter's expertise in designing, constructing and operating some of the world's largest aquariums. Brett has taken on the role of Project Manager of the Noah's Ark Aquarium.

Designs will be geared to endangered species that are found for relocation, working closely with

Figure 106 Brett Raymer, AMC Global

Figure 107 Anthony Mark Carter, AMC Global

critically endangered. Also threatened or endangered are whale sharks, Florida manatee, Galapagos penguins, sea turtles, sea otters, blue whales, river dolphins, gharials, polar bears and many more.

AMC Global

With all of that in mind, Noah's Ark approached co-owner of AMC Global Brett Raymer, best known in

international researchers and conservationists as well as developing expertise in the local community. Various stages will be accommodated in the conservation of species, from rescue and recovery, to their ultimate release in protected areas.

Brett Raymer, AMC Global:

"More than a thousand years ago – the common people shared a strange belief. They believed the world was as the gods willed it, and in order for it to change, it needed a champion. A champion either made or chosen by the gods themselves. We have come a long way since then. Beliefs of a set-in-stone destiny have been scattered to the wind, for we know now. Amidst the chaos of our constantly developing new world, we have the blade of courage to cut, and carve our own destiny. This is an ideology we share at AMC global; we are only limited by our own imagination.

Figure 108 Jellyfish

Brett Raymer, a man known for his commitment to both wildlife and sea life, once had a dream of riding the genesis flood. A thought of terror for most, yet a dream come true to some of his nature. Some would fear the massive waves blocking out the sun, and others like himself would jump at the chance of seeing not one, but two of every creature the world has to offer. A man who sees past the iron curtain man has set for themselves, and envisions a world of eco green harmony. A world where man is no longer disconnected from nature around him, but becomes one with the neighbours which inhabit his green and blue borders. Where humanity is no longer alone, but surrounded by the outstanding beauty of our nature's brothers and sisters. He works tirelessly to bridge a connection, from man to wild and sea life.

Anthony Mark Carter has been involved in numerous forms of entertainment including American E-sports. If Brett's passion for wildlife and sea life would be the first impact, Anthony would be an unstoppable force of forged sheer will behind it. He is a calculated veteran in achieving what the people of previous ages deemed impossible. When others tell him that it cannot be done, he formulates the means to bring that dream to reality. Through planning and creative thinking, no mountain is too high and no valley is too low. His intuition is only rivalled by his iron will to complete any given task to the best of his understanding. He is the engine, which runs on passion for creation.

Figure 109 IUCN endangered red list: Hammerhead Shark, Manta Ray

Figure 110 Sea Turtles, some species are on the IUCN endangered red list

As all of us, alone we are capable of very little. Yet some like them come together and forge a double-edged blade in which they too decide to carve a path to a better tomorrow. This is what brought them to the Noah's Ark project. Brett's excitement could not fathom the idea of a single aquarium housing so many different species, while Anthony could not wait to take on the challenge of making such an impossible feat a reality. We know it will not be effortless, yet we jump at the chance to take the road less travelled. To not only create an aquarium but to create an underwater world, where countless people can experience the wealth of life hidden beneath our shores. A place where people can not only see, but understand the bigger picture. We hope that through this grand scheme, others might realize the threat of pollution in our oceans. Years from now when the common people take a stand against polluting the ocean, let them say it started here.

The path ahead would certainly be difficult, yet as Lao Tzu said 'The journey of a thousand miles begins with a single step'. We know we can make this a reality. As we introduced to the people of Cape Town, and all those who it flocked together, the magnificence of the Two Oceans Aquarium. Where we not only displayed our team's excellent skillset, but gave our heart to ensure the aquarium residents would experience the big blue ocean to a whole new level. Each tank not only houses the necessary space which the species need to thrive, we put in the effort to ensure that they are comfortable. Creating an environment which simulates that of the deep ocean itself. For in the end, it's not just about these creatures' survival, so the people of the future can be in their presence. To us, they're beings all to themselves, and we hope to provide and nurture them to the best of our knowledge. For they do not represent entertainment, they represent a whole other world full of science and aquatic understanding. And by creating these exhibits we broaden the scientific intake of all who come to bear witness to their existence.

The Noah's Ark Project our top priority

However, pollution and global warming is a harsh reality few of humanity have yet to realise. Day by day these aquatic creatures' numbers dwindle, and will eventually be driven to extinction. This is why we at AMC Global have set our goals toward the Noah's Ark Project as our top priority. Housing and conserving these creatures would ensure their survival, even while our planet reaches a terraforming state. It would give us the necessary time to protect these species, while inspiring the world to take notice of these endangered creatures. Which in turn would hopefully create a snowball of possibilities, which will eventually lead to a cleaner and better tomorrow for not only sea and wildlife, but a better future for all.

We plan to not only display these magnificent creatures but to make visitors feel a part of the world we plan to design. Using acrylic clear tunnels, completely submerged by the blue beauty. Through this concept individuals can feel immersed in the sea life but also experience the presence of endangered species like never before. Resort accommodation, where guests can stay, would increase that exposure to conservation. Ensuring the possibility that individuals of all shapes, sizes and cultures would flock to the epicentre, where all sea life is conserved. Technology which was once nature's greatest threat, can turn the tide and create a great experience which would have visitors walk among sea life in a glorious augmented reality, along with various technological advancements. An idea for a world which is not only educational and entertaining, but a world which transports anyone caught in it to a whole new dimension of understanding.

Yet a haven of this calibre does not come without its challenges. To pursue and humanely capture these beauties, to replicate the worlds they knew to be their homes would be no easy task. It would require experts in a lot of fields, including logistics and marine biology. This will also grant these gifted individuals a chance to be a part of something greater. Who, I am certain, would jump sky-high if they are given the chance.

Unite individuals of all races, tribes and religion

We as human beings have all indulged in nature in some form or another. Some have indulged without even knowing the repercussions. What makes us want to give it our all, in the end, is not about conservation alone but something even greater. This place we intend to construct would mean nothing if it did not send a flashing message to those caught in its glare. More than conservation, it would serve as a beacon to those who still have hope in humanity, and a beacon of hope to those who believe nothing can be done. A beacon which will unite individuals of all races, tribes and religion to take a stand to build a better tomorrow.

That's what makes us want to give it our all, we have realised that we have taken an extravagant amount from nature and we are prepared to give it all back. In the form of one of the greatest conservations and philosophical projects this world has yet to experience. Something that would be remembered and revered as one of humanity's greatest triumphs."

Figure 111 Penguins, some species are on the IUCN endangered red list

Architecture & Development: Preserving Life on Earth while also Conceptualising Life Extra-Terrestrially

Noah's Ark must be the showcase of new and developing technologies in saving species, harmlessly and with absolute certainty.

That might not sound so futuristic, fantastical even, if we look at what is on the cards. Expending resources on technological advances for space colonisation, when those resources could better be employed in saving our planet and species. "One of the major environmental concerns of our time is the increasing consumption of Earth's resources to sustain our way of life. As more and more nations make the climb up from agricultural to industrial nations, their standard of life will improve, which will mean that more and more people will be competing for the same resources. While NASA spinoffs and other inventions can allow us to be more thrifty with Earth's resources, we nevertheless must come to grips with the problem that humanity is currently limited to one planet." – NASA

It's time we finally left the planetary womb

There are those who have already given up on our planet. "Humanity has been openly flirting with cosmic destiny for centuries. From the early reaches of our science fiction literature to the astounding feats of manned space exploration. We're getting anxious still wading on the earthen shores. The vast expanse of space is calling.

It's time we finally left the planetary womb and started strutting our stuff permanently amongst the stars.

But, in order to do that, we are going to need some serious new inventions for space colonisation. The likes of which will allow us to reach our most ascendent of aspirations — the conquering of the stars.

Whether it's getting to the moon first, crafting new terraformed sands of Mars, or spinning through self-sustaining colonies — the end result will be the same.

We're leaving the sandbox and these are some of the tools we'll use to do it." – Big Think

"In the 1970s, Princeton physicist Gerard K. O'Neill, was tasked with designing a free-floating space colony with existing technology, materials and construction techniques. Suffice to say, we're no closer to having space colonies now than we were then. O'Neill wrote a number of fascinating books on the topic and claimed that the concept was feasible at the time. He was interested in building alternative human habitats that were both beyond Earth and beyond a planetary body. Out of this was conceived the idea of a giant rotating spaceship, which could support a biosphere and house up to 10 million people.

This space colonisation concept has come to be known, after its founder, as the O'Neill Cylinder. The basis of the structure would be crafted out of steel and aluminium and formed into a hollow cylinder. This kind of settlement is arguably the most important of inventions we'd need to give us a permanent place in space.

O'Neill's plans for the colonies originally appeared in the journal *Physics Today*. He went on to expand on the idea in a number of books, most notably in *The High Frontier: Human Colonies in Space*. A closed ecosystem inside would create the biosphere. Sunlight and solar power would be utilized by giant glass windows in space. Altogether the goal would be to create a climate-controlled living space. There would be no limit to what kind of climate or ecosystem you wanted to create.

Rather than living on top of a sphere as we do now, future cylinder colonists would settle on the inside. Artificial gravity would be created by the cylinder's walls rotating. These colonies would be situated at Lagrange points in order to stay in a consistent and stable gravitational environment. It would take weeks to fly to these colonies from Earth.

It's mind-boggling to think of the number of inventions needed for a project of this magnitude. But humanity has never shied away from inventing insane and impossible things. An entire space mining industry would be needed to transport rocky material from the moon and asteroids, to serve as the bedrock for these colonies. Space construction crews would assemble the colonies in space, backed by the thoughtful minds of engineers, master ecologists and so on.

Our American Gilded Age would look pathetically poor in comparison to such an expedition.

George S Boughton C Eng conceived of a similar space colonisation in his book *DeepStorm OutTack* (published in 2012). Except his starting point was far more practical. Significantly smaller cylinders, with more realistic populations in the thousands, would be built one at a time and anchored together electronically. The colony would grow to form the Near Earth Territories, commencing as early as the 2060's, using materials mined on the moon. He rated any idea of colonising elsewhere, anywhere outside of orbiting the Earth, as simply beyond real science. Venturing blindly anywhere external to the solar system, at distances even out of reach of any communications, would make no sense at all. And any small planetary surfaces in the Solar System, Mars included, would offer nothing to accommodate the billions who will very shortly be overpopulating the Earth. Solving that overpopulation, along with saving nature, is what everyone must rather put their minds on.

A new human breed

Interestingly, *OutTack's* Near Earth Territories were populated predominantly by young professionals, who were of necessity raised from designer babies. They were a new human breed specifically adapted to live and work permanently in space, since only the cylinders' outer layers had Earth gravity. The same would apply to colonists anywhere else off this world, Earth.

Space colonisation technology such as O'Neill's was recently referenced by none other than Jeff Bezos, the CEO of Amazon. A student of science fiction and fact, Bezos's goal is to help build the future of our space industry and one day make something like this possible. Only time will tell if he's up to the task.

Bezos did recently get some flack from flim flam man, Elon Musk — who is more concerned with getting to Mars in the next five years… or never. Now, if Musk would have read up a little on his literature, he'd have realised he's an unwitting planetary chauvinist — a term coined by legendary fiction writer Isaac Asimov. During an interview, Asimov was questioned about whether or not he'd ever written about space colonies. His response: "We've all been planet chauvinists. We've all believed people should live on the surface of a planet, of a world. I've had colonies on the moon — so have a hundred other science fiction writers. The closest I came to a manufactured world in free space was to suggest that we go out to the asteroid belt and hollow out the asteroids, and make ships out of them [in the novelette *The Martian Way*]. It never occurred to me to bring the material from the asteroids in towards the earth, where conditions are pleasanter, and build the worlds there."

"Yet, there is still some validity in wanting to both colonise planets such as Mars and create free floating space colonies." – Big Think

But looking at all of this technology being developed and used to move us so we can live amongst the stars, why can't we realise that we are already living amongst the stars. Moving from one planet to another will not necessarily solve the problem for our future generations.

No, it is very much up to us to ensure that we use all tools available for making our current situation better, not only for us but our future generations. We need to apply what we know, to our here and now. It is up to us to make that change and use technology we know of, as well as technology still in development, to paint a new rainbow. It will be hard but not impossible.

Animal Conservation

Animal conservation, or more specifically wildlife conservation, is Noah's Ark's ultimate goal. The objective being to sustainably conserve every living species in the world. But where did wildlife conservation start?

Wildlife conservation includes all of man's efforts to preserve wild animals and plants and save them from extinction

Before The Noah's Ark Foundation can even think of embarking on a project like this, we first need to understand where it all started and why. An article 'You Ask Andy' answered exactly this question. "Wildlife conservation includes all of man's efforts to preserve wild animals and plants and save them from extinction. The first game reserves were set up by rulers of ancient civilisations as ways to protect their own personal hunting grounds. It became a practice that was continued by the medieval kings of Europe."

Who knew that conservation started that far back in the day? Did leaders of the time know we would face problems concerning the preservation of wildlife, or what was the motivator behind their implementations?

The answer to the question continues to explain that: "Realising that it was important to protect wildlife so that game would be available in future years, laws were passed by the British colonies during the 1600s and 1700s to limit hunting. Unfortunately, most of the colonists ignored these laws.

It wasn't until the late 1800s that effective wildlife conservation in Canada and the United States was started.

The world's first national park was established by Congress in 1872. It is Yellowstone National Park which lies in the northwest corner of Wyoming and spreads into Idaho and Montana.

Also during the late 1800s, many of the states began to pass and enforce game laws. And during the 1890s, millions of acres of forest land were protected by the national forest system.

Then in 1903, President Theodore Roosevelt established the nation's first federal wildlife refuge on Pelican Island in Florida.

The national park system wasn't set up by Congress until 1916. It was then under the direction of the National Park Service, an agency of the Department of the Interior.

The government created the Fish and Wildlife Service in 1940 in the same department to strengthen the wildlife conservation programme. The service manages the federal wildlife refuges, which in 1966 were organised into the National Wildlife Refuge System.

Canada created its first park, Banff National Park, in 1887.

Figure 112 Banff National Park, Canada

Figure 113 A giraffe

Sabie Game Reserve, which is now Kruger National Park, was established in what is now South Africa in 1898. Now an extensive network of parks and reserves protects African wildlife.

Palaeontologists tell us that various species had become extinct even before people appeared on the Earth. However, in the past species evolved to replace those that died off, and the total variety of life did not diminish.

Today, human activities unfortunately kill off species with no hope for their replacement. Wildlife conservation, therefore, became very important.

Since 1600, various species of wildlife have become extinct in North America including the Carolina parakeet, the passenger pigeon, the California grizzly bear, the Florida black wolf, the Franklinia tree of Georgia and a birch that once grew in Virginia.

Care must be taken since several hundreds of species of animals and thousands of species of plants even now face the danger of extinction. Included are such animals as the Asiatic lion, the Bengal tiger, the blue whale, the whooping crane, the California condor, the ivory billed woodpecker and all the Asian rhinoceroses.

Plants facing extinction include the black cabbage tree, the Ozark chestnut, the St Helena redwood, several kinds of California manzanitas and the frankincense tree of Africa."

So there we have it. Ancient leaders knew how important it was to protect and preserve wildlife. But if they knew it, why is it so hard for humanity to comprehend now? Or are we jumping the gun and assuming too much? Yes, there might be those who understand and care but the general consensus in developed countries is that most that know don't care enough to do something about it. In developing countries they're too concerned about job security to even think about it.

People are aware of conferences or summits when governments discuss these issues and agree to do something, so why should we be concerned?

Enforce protection of lands allocated as nature reserves

Progress has been made, with UN Biodiversity targets agreed in Aichi. President Trump pulled the USA out and now President Biden is re-engaging the USA. With that new resolve, governments will meet this year to set targets beyond the 2011 to 2020 period agreed, also addressing targets not met (most of them) and agreeing on measures to enforce protection of the lands allocated as nature reserves (30% across the world).

So the newsflash is that governments have taken the threat of climate change seriously with instigating measures to reduce carbon emissions and footprints.

Figure 114 African elephant

Figure 115 African wildlife, Noah's Ark series 1 (2 photos)

Now they have to get behind targets to also save wildlife. They know how interlinked it all is, how vital biodiversity is to dealing with climate change. But what it will really take, is for people everywhere, in all countries, to raise their voices and demand action.

A green culture change across the world

It's time for that culture change, a green culture change, among all people of the world.

All the more reason, right now, for Noah's Ark to effectively and confidently step forward and say: We are not only here to make the change but ready for you to do the same.

According to World Animal Protection, the pangolin is the most poached wildlife in the world with only an estimate of 50,000 pangolins left. But, as of 2018, there were only between 27,000 and 30,000 rhinos left.

Every single one of us can participate to clean up our act and take our beautiful planet back to her former glory. No one is saying this is easy, but it most certainly is possible if people everywhere help within their immediate surroundings and circumstances.

The Human Carbon Footprint

The impact of climate change on our biodiversity is not only real but very severe, so what we can and must do is change our mindsets about the carbon footprint we leave behind.

Action on Climate Change

Individual action can include personal choices in many areas, such as: diet, the means of long and short distance travel, household energy use, consumption of goods and services, and family size. Individuals can also engage in local and political advocacy, even join marches, around issues of climate change.

The challenge is great though with much yet to learn, about how the planet functions and the part that biodiversity plays. As stewards, now, we have a moral duty of care to nature. In effect we are guardians of nature. A responsibility that we must not fail in. The consequences otherwise are unimaginable, and could even be catastrophic. Not only for our wildlife but humans too.

Noah's Ark does not have all the answers. At the very least it will give our animals a fighting chance at survival, with experts on location to research the effects of climate change and what exactly we can do to change and reverse them.

Technological advances are in development around the world to combat climate change, with exceptionally gifted scientists and researchers leading the way. Technology has also been a big contributor to the problem, with influencing declines in wildlife, and now it is time for it to play a major role in reversing the effects.

These are some innovations in development, extracted from SkyNews.com, that could very well play a big role in our future.

1. Carbon Capture

The rise in the average temperature, of the Earth, is primarily blamed by scientists on man-made emissions of greenhouse gases, trapping radiation in the atmosphere that otherwise would escape into space.

Among the most significant is carbon dioxide (CO_2), concentrations which have increased by almost 50% since the industrial revolution began.

Innovations include carbon capture, utilisation and storage, the Net Zero Teesside (NZT) project being an interesting example.

NZT aims to capture CO_2 produced in industrial processes and powerplants, and transport it by pipeline

Figure 116 Team meeting, Noah's Ark on Afternoon Express ZA

Figure 117 Research on endangered species & habitats

Figure 118 Richard & Hein in Waterberg Predator Park

Figure 119 Richard with Riana Van Nieuwenhuizen at Cheetah Experience Conservation Project

to offshore storage strata several kilometres beneath the North Sea. Secured there, it might be synthesised into new fuels in the future.

The aim, as the NZT project's name suggests, will be to reduce carbon emissions in a number of carbon-intensive industries in the North East (UK) to zero by as early as 2030.

But the scale of the Earth's problem is far more significant than can be solved by the selective decarbonisation of a low number of businesses.

2. Feeding Cows Seaweed

Another significant greenhouse gas is methane, emissions of which are reaching record levels in cattle farming.

Agriculture accounted for roughly two-thirds of all methane emissions related to human activities between 2000 and 2017 according to a recent study, with fossil fuels contributing most of the remaining third.

The methane emissions in question primarily come from burping cattle. It's a result of how cows digest food – fermenting it in their stomachs where the sugars are converted into simpler molecules that can be absorbed by the body.

Scientists have discovered that a red seaweed which grows in the tropics can reduce methane emissions by 80% in cows when it is added as a supplement to their feed.

However, with nearly 1.5 billion head of cattle globally, there is simply not enough of this seaweed currently available to suppress these burps – although perhaps some scientists might be able to reproduce the crucial ingredient which will help to keep them down.

3. Delicious Insects

While the dietary decisions of individuals don't normally come within the purview of potential technological solutions to climate change, innovative food creation definitely does.

Another interesting way to reduce the methane pollution from cattle farming, would be to replace beef with a substitute made from insects – and this is already taking off in places. Protein-rich insects such as mealworms can be farmed without the demands put

Figure 120 Climate Change flooding – from *Dennis to Alice*, George S Boughton

on land or water by cattle farming. Apart from the high protein content of insects, there are a number of other crucial nutrients which humans generally only find in meat – including iron.

Some scientific research suggests that a range of insects could provide all of the mineral nutrients humans need. But, of course, even this isn't a quick fix. Insect burgers largely remain a novelty item rather than something which can be mass produced and consumed.

4. Climate Repair

The Centre for Climate Repair at the University of Cambridge is investigating a number of ideas for repairing the damage done by human pollution.

Among their ideas are refreezing the poles by brightening the clouds above them, essentially by spraying tiny drops of salt into the sky to assist the clouds in reflecting radiation back into space. Another suggestion has been 'greening' the oceans, essentially fertilising them to encourage the growth of plant matter and algae to absorb more CO_2.

However, some research warns that this could cause enormous disruption to the oceans' ecosystems, and potentially wouldn't even then be able to capture enough CO_2 to offset emissions.

Figure 121 Cows on a farm in the UK

Figure 122 Working from home

5. Remote Working

As the **coronavirus** pandemic has shown, many office jobs can be successfully fulfilled from home – potentially offering a route to reduce emissions from transport and office buildings.

Driving to and from work is the largest source of carbon emissions in the developed world.

The technology to support remote working has been rapidly adopted as businesses attempt to manage the impact of **COVID-19** on their workers, and governments rush to lock down their countries and prevent mass deaths.

However remote working may only be an effective method of reducing emissions during the summer.

It turns out that when buildings need to be heated during the winter it is much more efficient to have numerous people in a single building rather than distributed across their own homes. Some research suggests this might even offset the reductions of emissions from transportation.

6. Greater use of Data Centres

A similar logic regarding the heating of individual homes versus office buildings can be applied when it comes to computation.

The advent of computers has increased electricity consumption considerably, but modern data centres are often far more energy efficient than personal computers. Rather than performing energy-intensive applications on local machines – from crunching complicated numbers through to playing video games – people could begin to offset a considerable amount of that energy by having these applications performed in the cloud. The big technology companies which specialise in providing cloud computing services – Amazon, Google and Microsoft – are large consumers of renewable energy. Google and Microsoft have both launched cloud gaming platforms too which don't require gamers to purchase consoles (the production of which also causes emissions) to play them.

However, data centres are dependent upon quality internet connections, which themselves can produce emissions, and for many people across the world those connections simply are not available.

Figure 123 Data centre

7. Household Energy Efficiency

The single-most effective technological solution to climate change is going to be reducing energy consumption overall, and nothing is going to do that more than making homes more energy efficient. The technology to achieve this is already there, with many of the newest products on the market capable of shaving hundreds of pounds off of household bills annually.

The European Union (EU) has established an energy labelling scheme for how energy efficient appliances are, informing consumers about how much it will cost them to run refrigerators and washing machines as well as other products from light bulbs to televisions.

Energy savings made through design innovations for these household goods might be small individually, but they have the potential to scale up and significantly impact energy consumption across the course of a year for a household, and even more significantly across all households in a country.

Across the EU, buildings consume 40% of overall energy and are responsible for 35% of CO_2 emissions – although energy consumption per household has dropped over the past 50 years due to efficiency measures.

Figure 124 Energy efficient light bulbs

But according to the independent statutory body, the Committee on Climate Change, homes in the UK are "unfit" at the moment to meet the challenges posed by warming global temperatures and the need to reduce energy consumption. Newer, greener, electronic goods could be a good place to start.

So, there you have it. These are just seven ways we could adapt and change according to Sky News, and they do all look fairly reasonable.

Community Meets Conservation

However small it might seem to you as an Individual just remember: the smallest of things usually has the biggest outcome. You can help to save animal life by doing the simplest of things.

Keep changes small, it will still have an outcome and a positive effect, as long as we start somewhere.

Have a look at this Sky News article.

Having said this, wildlife conservation does not come without its own challenges and obstacles.

Habitats are under a tremendous threat due to human intervention. It has become more and more difficult to protect these habitats within conservancies as poachers are increasingly willing to risk their lives just to provide for their families.

Devastating effect on populations of rhinos, elephants and other charismatic megafauna

Wildlife trade has always been a big issue, throughout the world, and we don't really know the full extent of it. According to Fauna & Flora International, illegal wildlife trade has become a high-profile issue receiving global media attention, not least because of its devastating effect on populations of rhinos, elephants and other charismatic megafauna. But its impact on geckos, orchids, seahorses and numerous other species is equally alarming.

They go on to say that many forms of wildlife can be legally and sustainably harvested and traded. Traditionally, much of this trade has taken place at local levels, but globalisation has opened up new markets and an increasing volume of wildlife is now traded internationally. The trade takes many forms, encompassing live animals and ornamental plants, pharmaceutical ingredients, leathers, skins and furs, collectible specimens and high-value timber.

Noah's Ark is in no way saying it knows all the answers, but surely poachers and traders are not in this for fun. It is extremely difficult to make an honest living today, especially in Africa, and in small communities people are often faced with an offer to conduct wrong-doing to earn some money.

That of course is not news but very often, and especially in the smaller rural communities, starvation and poor living conditions are the driving force behind poaching.

Figure 125 Richard with Tembe Traditional Council Elders

With the new Noah's Ark project, we are looking to minimise that need, by providing the community with proper infrastructure, training and necessary skills that would enable them to not only work on the Noah's Ark project, but also allow them to find work after the completion of the park, should The Noah's Ark Foundation not be in a position to keep them employed.

By investing in local communities, as well as local issues around the world with the life-boat programme, we are also investing in the welfare of our wildlife.

The less need there is to poach and trade, the more we save wildlife. But it does start with us and we need to make the change. This will be extremely hard as poaching and trading have become such a career these past few decades, that it is the only thing many poor communities know how to do.

Noah's Ark will simply have to take away and or reduce poverty, and that can only be achieved with the help of the world, and by providing proper care and job creation.

We simply cannot exist without wildlife

The Noah's Ark team, together with the project will revolutionise the way the world looks at conservation, preservation and sustainability. This project is very much needed, especially now that we have encountered COVID-19. It gave a new perspective on life and what we must do to ensure the survival of our planet and what she holds. The pandemic has given the world a chance to reflect, evaluate, and measure the standards. As one planet we have come to the realisation that we cannot exist alone and that everything is inter-linked.

We simply cannot exist without our wildlife, which is the reason we need to protect and preserve, rather than hunt and trade.

The project will give The Noah's Ark Foundation the perfect opportunity to investigate problematic areas around the world and, together with the relevant authorities, communities, and legislative channels, implement effective programmes dealing with those specific areas.

This is a necessity, as we are not dealing with this alone but as a planet; populations are facing the same issues around the world when it comes to wildlife conservation. And it is becoming harder than ever to protect these habitats, as humans look to expand their territories regardless that their strategies are invasive. We are already running out of space with regards to elephant populations globally, due to humans taking more space without regard for the wildlife inhabiting it. Many will argue that culling is the solution, but is it really? Can't we rather look to rehoming before we turn to the most evil solution? The answer unfortunately is very often 'no'.

That is because many conservancies simply do not want elephant or any other additional wildlife for that matter, as they have their own internal capacity issues. This is something The Noah's Ark Foundation can work on now, while the park is still in development, with looking to work with current conservancies and rehome wildlife where possible.

Figure 126 Christina on community work in KZN

Climate Change & Biodiversity

So, as mentioned, climate change plays a big role in biodiversity but just how much exactly?

Well, *Sciencing* puts it very clearly. "As climate change alters temperature and weather patterns, it will also impact plant and animal life.

Scientists expect the number and range of species, which define biodiversity, will decline greatly as temperatures continue to rise. The loss of biodiversity could have many negative impacts on the future of ecosystems and humanity worldwide." Climate change also has a huge effect on the environment, as *Sciencing* explains: "Greenhouse gases, such as carbon dioxide, absorb heat from sunlight, preventing it from escaping back into space.

As the level of greenhouse gases rises, so will temperatures. The Intergovernmental Panel on Climate Change predicts that by 2100, temperatures may rise as much as 6 degrees Celsius (11 degrees Fahrenheit).

Though the Earth's climate has changed in the past, the rapid severity of this change will directly affect ecosystems and biodiversity."

But what are the effects on biodiversity? Well, seeing as we are not the experts, we have to turn to them and see what they say.

What *Sciencing* is saying is that it has an effect on both land and sea biodiversity. "Rising temperatures already affect the world's polar regions. Diminishing ice packs reduce the habitats of polar bears, penguins, puffins and other Arctic creatures. As the ice melts, it increases the sea level, which will affect and perhaps destroy ecosystems on coastlines. Changes in temperatures will also cause shifts in mating cycles, especially for migratory animals that rely on changing seasons to indicate their migration and reproductive timing."

Upset the biodiversity in the Earth's waters

"Rising sea levels" on the other hand, "will also cause changes to ocean temperatures and perhaps even currents. Such changes would have a strong impact on zooplankton, an essential part of the food chain in the ocean. Shifts in where plankton live and how big the size of their populations could upset the biodiversity in the Earth's waters. Whales, especially, could bear the brunt of this, as many whale species require mass amounts of plankton to survive. In addition, increased carbon dioxide causes acidification of the ocean, affecting creatures and plants that are sensitive to pH imbalances."

Figure 127 Sea corals dying (photo: Peta Photography)

Figure 128 Climate change, endangered: polar bears

Figure 129 Climate change, wildfires

Temperatures in South African cities

City	Summer JANUARY				Winter JULY			
Average max/min	MAXIMUM		MINIMUM		MAXIMUM		MINIMUM	
Celsius/Fahrenheit	C	F	C	F	C	F	C	F
Bloemfontein	31	88	15	59	17	63	-2	28
Cape Town	26	79	16	61	18	64	7	45
Durban	28	82	21	70	23	73	11	52
East London	26	79	18	64	21	70	10	50
George	25	77	15	59	19	66	7	45
Johannesburg	26	79	15	59	20	68	4	39
Kimberley	33	91	18	64	19	66	3	37
Mthatha	27	81	16	61	21	70	4	39
Musina	34	93	21	70	25	77	7	45
Nelspruit	29	84	19	66	23	73	6	43
Pietermaritzburg	28	82	18	64	23	73	3	37
Polokwane	28	82	17	63	20	68	4	39
Port Elizabeth	25	77	18	64	20	68	9	48
Pretoria	29	84	18	64	24	75	5	41
Richards Bay	29	84	21	70	23	73	12	54
Skukuza	33	91	21	70	26	79	6	43
Thohoyandou	31	88	20	68	24	75	10	50
Upington	36	97	20	68	21	70	4	39

DATA SOURCE: SOUTH AFRICAN WEATHER SERVICE

Figure 130 Temperatures in South Africa

Figure 131 KwaZulu-Natal ZA, Noah's Ark s1 ep2

As biodiversity decreases, disruptions in the food chain may affect humanity's ability to feed an ever-growing population

But then *Sciencing* goes on, saying that the lack of biodiversity is far worse than we might think. "As biodiversity decreases, there will be far-reaching effects. Disruptions in the food chain may greatly affect not only ecosystems but also humanity's ability to feed an ever-growing population. For example, losing diverse insect species will decrease plant pollination. Additionally, this may decrease humanity's ability to produce medicine, as extinction claims more and more key plant species. Biodiversity also protects against natural disasters, such as grasses that have evolved specifically to resist the spread of wildfires."

What does this mean for Noah's Ark? Well, this means that we would need to work with the best of the best to ensure that we have the correct balance needed between climate and biodiversity. This might sound easier than it is but really this would be a massive task with the GeoDomes alone, home to wildlife of the Amazon rainforest as well as the polar bears. Because Noah's Ark would bring in wildlife from around the world, we would need to make absolutely sure that we have the correct balance.

The South African climate is not suitable for most wildlife of the world, it can get extremely hot, but it is home to the famous big five as well as other indigenous wildlife which luckily can survive under the African sun. What will be problematic is sea life and some wildlife not indigenous to South Africa, for which Noah's Ark is planning climate controlled GeoDomes. The technology that will go into making these is phenomenal, including some that is still in development, with the aim of having a balanced biodiversity that is key to each habitat.

In South Africa, or more particularly Africa, climate change has been severe not only on wildlife but humans too. The World Wildlife Foundation (WWF) reported that: "Semi-arid areas of the Sahel, the Kalahari, and the Karoo historically have supported nomadic societies that migrate in response to annual and seasonal rainfall variations. Nomadic pastoral systems are intrinsically able to adapt to fluctuating and extreme climates, provided they have sufficient scope for movement and other necessary elements in the system remain in place.

However, the prolonged drying trend in the Sahel since the 1970s has demonstrated the vulnerability of such groups to climate change: they cannot simply move their axis of migration when the wetter end already is densely occupied and permanent water points fail at the drier end. The result has been widespread loss of human life and livestock, and substantial changes to the social system."

A race against time to save at least some species on this beautiful Earth

So, not only are animals affected but all life is. Noah's Ark is in a race against time to save at least some species on this beautiful Earth.

The WWF also reported that "Africa occupies about one-fifth of the global land surface and contains about one-fifth of all known species of plants, mammals, and birds in the world, as well as one-sixth of amphibians and reptiles (Siegfried 1989). Climate change has already affected the marine animals of Africa. Coral reefs in the Indian Ocean experienced massive bleaching in 1998, with over 50% mortality in some regions (Spalding 2001). Damage to coral reef systems has far reaching implications for fisheries, food security, tourism and overall marine biodiversity."

Of course this would mean that Noah's Ark will have to be very careful when it comes to planning the aquarium. As we now know, there are a lot of intriguing but also scary factors to consider when planning an aquarium of this scale where you want to have as many marine species as possible.

The conservation plan going in to this project would have to be absolutely flawless and on point as we do not want to do more harm than good when planning these mega structures.

South Africa in general has a vast pool of talent and experts in climate change, some of whom are world renowned. Noah's Ark will take on these experts to help guide and support the project, so as to steer it in the right direction when it comes to climate change and biodiversity, so that we don't make any mistakes.

Figure 132 Climate change, lizard in drought

But it does not only rely on local talent. There are climate experts in their respective fields that will be involved in planning and execution stages of the project, from around the world. Climate change has over the past decades become a huge global concern, with the first issue of climate change brought before the US Senate on 23 June, 1988. Since then, more scientists started focussing their expertise and fields on climate change and global warming, and how that affects our planet.

South Africa generally has warm weather, as previously mentioned, and that usually comes paired with extreme drought in some areas of the country. Just recently Cape Town came through a three-year drought that left the city devastated and crushed by the affects. Due to the drought, some measures were taken on water restrictions and as a result, had an adverse effect on tourism in the region.

Strong rains in June 2018 luckily led to dam levels rising to 70% capacity and saved the city from 'day zero', a reference to when the major supply to dam levels would be less than 13.5%. It will take the city a while to recover economically, of course, and one cannot eliminate the likelihood of this happening again – especially with the ever-increasing damage that climate change is doing to the country and it being so unpredictable.

The perfect climate

Scientists have predicted less rainfall for South Africa, with extreme and prolonged heat waves periodically as a result of climate change. In consequence, Noah's Ark will be built in an area with normal cycles of annual rainfall. But the reason for choosing the area is far more important than rainfall, even though water supply plays a vital role. KwaZulu-Natal on the south east of the country, has the perfect climate identified for most of the land animals indigenous to the country, as well as some other world's species. The area has been identified with minimum migration patterns; which would obviously be beneficial to Noah's Ark, as there should be minimum disruption to the habitats of animals we'd look to house there.

Incidentally, KwaZulu-Natal was also home to a Climate Change Summit in 2019, between the 14th and 15th August, where delegates were expected to craft a clear programme to respond to the ever-growing threat of inclement weather conditions caused by climate change.

This came as no surprise, as KwaZulu-Natal over the last couple of years had some extreme rainfall and weather changes, which is very unusual for the area. This had a major impact on the plant and wildlife species in the area. Some plant species, not used to and not needing so much water to survive, drowned while leaving some wildlife without food to survive. While other plants thrived with the increase in rainfall and along with certain wildlife.

In contrast to Cape Town, there is no shortage of water which is beneficial to the biodiversity of the KwaZulu-Natal region.

See also Planning and Environmental Impact Assessments.

Figure 133 Elephants crossing a river

Technology

To build this massive undertaking, we need to look at how to conserve wildlife.

Noah's Ark will create an environment, in effect a home, for specimens of every living species in the world. No problem there, for wildlife that can readily acclimatise. For that which cannot, climate-controlled GeoDomes will be especially designed.

Technology will be the answer for the whole park, from infrastructure and energy, to sustainability, entertainment, waste management and transportation. As mentioned earlier, some of the technology is in development. And as we will need that for the climate-controlled GeoDomes as well as the park defence systems, the best thing would be to involve those scientists in the planning stages. Thereby, we can provide them with the infrastructure to implement the technology when the time is right. The park will be heavily protected. As you can imagine, it would otherwise be a one stop shopping mall for hunters and poachers, defeating the whole purpose of protecting and conserving wildlife.

Luckily that technology will be needed in the last phase of the project, which means the project can go ahead with the main buildings and functions as planned.

In 2015, the Connected Conservation project was launched at a conservation facility adjacent to the Kruger National Park in South Africa. The 24-hour round-the-clock surveillance system they installed, proved effective in reducing rhino poaching by 96% within the first two years.

Poachers however, are becoming more and more sophisticated in their attempts and ways to poach, without being noticed and/or picked up on security systems. You will also find times when they are spotted but just don't care, as the need to survive and provide for their families is far greater than the risk of being caught.

Figure 134 Rhino horn (photo; Peta Photography)

Figure 135 Wind energy

Figure 136 Solar power

Noah's Ark will source more advanced security systems, capable of eliminating poaching risks entirely. Perimeter security will incorporate electromagnetic pulse beams, as African rhino poaching is mostly carried out by helicopter – believe it or not. It is absolutely shocking, the lengths that these poachers will go to in order to get what they want.

Renewable energy will be installed to power the park. Solutions under consideration range from wind turbines, to tidal and wave energy as well as geothermal energy and solar power.

Because of Africa's unique climate and the park's planned location, with a very close coastline of roughly five kilometres, any of these would be suitable depending on preferences, assessments and land surveys. The best options will be those that are eco-friendly and positive for the park environment.

Noah's Ark's technology strategy extends to a fleet of driverless vehicles, to transport visitors between the reception management building, the eco-friendly train and wherever they want to go. Within the Visitor Centre and Leisure Complex area as well as the GeoDomes area, all transport other than safari vehicles will be fully autonomous.

Figure 137 Autonomous Vehicle

Building an Ark

Lessons from Noah

I have always loved a good action story; be it a movie, a book or my Uncle Diffy (short for "difficult", don't ask) after a couple of beers. And, as a kid I had a particular fondness for stories from the Old Testament. They were generally simple, optimistic, action-oriented and involved great feats; like a man commanding the sun to stand still at the height of battle… and it did. Never mind that, technically it's the earth that moves and not the sun.

But, I am already digressing… (it's a gift).

So the story goes: God sees that humanity has become too evil to live and decides to destroy everything in a flood. Suddenly, everyone and all the animals are on the endangered species list. But God has a plan for one man, his wife and kids, and a sample pair of every other living creature. Honestly, I would have left out mosquitoes, but that's just me.

And the details of said plan are quite simple: build a big boat (henceforth to be known as an "ark") and God will make rain. God will supply the layout and dimensions, what materials to use, where to place the door (there was only one, no windows), etc. And when the ark is built, animals will suddenly appear in pairs and enter the dark confines therein unbidden. I can't even get a puppy to sit.

And, as the old adage goes, history repeats itself.

Once again, we find ourselves called upon to save endangered animal species. Yes, we are Noah. The key differences this time:

 This is not a temporary flood event, so a more robust ark, that will last for as long as it takes, is required;

 Since we are made in God's image, we will supply the layouts and dimensions, what materials to use, where to place the doors and windows (thank goodness), etc;

 The animals will definitely not bring themselves to this ark;

 Also, animals seem to have developed a higher level of mortality since the days of Noah and just bringing a pair together will not guarantee their survival;

 Etc, etc.

Perhaps, the most telling difference for us at Jabulani Matobela Consultants (Pty) Ltd (JMC) is that a lot of Noahs will be involved at various levels. Noahs worked tirelessly to conceptualise the ark. Noahs are working on putting specifics to this concept. Noahs are required to sponsor the development. Noahs will be required to operate and maintain the facilities to be built…

And JMC is the Noah chosen to ensure that all the pieces fit together and nothing falls through the cracks – Project Management, in the vernacular.

We interpret our involvement on the Noah's Ark project as follows[1]:

---

1   Based on A Guide to the Project Management Body of Knowledge (PMBOK Guide), Sixth Edition.

Project Integration Management

Project Integration Management is the glue that brings all the pieces together and involves making choices about:

🦏	Resource allocation:	– who does what, when and how?
		– what material resources are required?
🦏	Balancing competing demands:	– the final product is required today but the individual pieces will take a lifetime to bring together; where is the optimum delivery time?
		– what can we afford?
🦏	Examining alternative approaches:	– have we considered our options fully?
		– is there another way?
🦏	Meeting project objectives:	– do we know where we are headed?
		– are we achieving what we set out to?
🦏	Managing interdependencies:	– are there cracks for things to fall through?
		– have we covered all the cracks adequately?

Project Scope Management

Project Scope Management ensures that the project includes all the work required, and only the work required, to complete the project successfully. This means defining what is and what is not included in the project.

Our Noah's Ark will comprise the following major developments:

(i) animal (and plant) sanctuary:
- accommodate all animal species on the endangered list
- provide for effective breeding programmes

(ii) science centre:
- undertake strategic research aimed at increasing the population growth of endangered species
- create effective measures to eradicate all human-related contributing factors to population decline
- strategically introduce endangered species into the natural ecosystem of the park on a regular basis

(iii) visitor centre:
- conference facilities
- hotels
- entertainment and food courts
- amusement facilities (water slides, etc.)
- museum
- clinics / health centre

(iv) bulk services provision:
- fresh / potable water supplies
- waste water treatment and disposal
- solid waste treatment and disposal
- electricity and energy supplies
- access roads network

(v) support services facilities:
- offices
- staff housing
- workshops
- goods receiving
- light aircraft facilities

(vi) other:
- pilot project

Project Schedule Management

Project Schedule Management is concerned with the timely completion of the project. This starts off with determining realistic timeframes for the performance of various tasks, working out dependencies between tasks, and consolidating the pieces into an overall Project Schedule. The result is a detailed plan that represents how and when the project will deliver the products, services and results as defined in the project scope.

The Project Schedule for the Noah's Ark Project is based on the following anticipated stages:

Project Stage	Description of Stage	Documents Generated
Stage 1: Initiation (Scoping)	Conceptual stage in which the broad project deliverables are explored and several options are generated. The full professional team is also constituted and mandated in their respective disciplines.	■ Inception report (this) ■ Appointment letters for the professional team ■ Discipline scoping reports
Stage 2: Concept and Viability	Preliminary design stage in which the various professionals evaluate conceptual options. Preferred options are prioritized, coordinated with other disciplines, selected and the viability of the project is more rigorously tested.	■ Preliminary design reports for each discipline ■ Preliminary budget estimates for each discipline (70% accurate)
Stage 3: Design Development	Detail design stage in which the selected options are more fully defined and their viability confirmed. The overall project solution is now fully defined in terms of cost, schedule, scope and other requirements.	■ Detail design reports ■ Bills of quantities for more accurate cost estimates
Stage 4: Documentation and Procurement	Procurement stage culminating in the appointment of suitably experienced and competent contractors. Where contractors are selected and / or nominated, rates are negotiated and project-specific performance contracts signed.	■ Contract documentation (appointments and SLAs) ■ Preliminary programmes of works
Stage 5: Construction	Execution stage in which the defined outcomes are delivered in line with the scope, schedule, cost, quality and other parameters.	■ Detailed programmes ■ Cashflow projections ■ Performance reports
Stage 6: Close-out	Contractual and financial project closure.	■ Completion certificates ■ CoCs ■ O & M Manuals ■ Final accounts

Project Cost Management

This involves, you guessed it: planning, estimating, budgeting, financing, funding, managing, and controlling costs so that the project can be completed within the approved budget.

Naturally, this is a sensitive area and we will hold off giving out figures until a satisfactory level of understanding of detail has been reached with stakeholders and role players. Suffice it to say, this is no mean feat and will cost a pretty penny.

Project Quality Management

Project Quality Management is concerned with planning, managing and controlling project and product quality requirements in order to meet stakeholders' objectives.

Quality will primarily be ensured by employing suitably qualified and industry registered professionals on the project team. This should ensure that the highest industry best practices standards are adhered to.

Project Resource Management

Project Resource Management includes the processes to identify, acquire and manage the resources needed for the successful completion of the project. The goal is to ensure that the right resources are available to the project at the right time and place. This process will be managed in conjunction with the certified professionals responsible for project designs.

Project Communications Management

Project Communications Management ensures effective information exchange, between stakeholders and role players, for the success of the project.

A system of reports, meetings and other communication media has been set up to ensure the effective sharing of pertinent project information.

Project Risk Management

Project Risk Management involves risk identification, analysis, response planning, response implementation and monitoring in order to decrease the probability and / or impact of negative risks so as to optimize the chances of project success.

This is an ongoing activity which involves regular brainstorming to identify and manage risks as they arise.

Project Procurement Management

Project Procurement Management includes the processes necessary to purchase or acquire products, services or results needed from outside the project team. This involves the development and administration of agreements such as contracts, purchase orders, memoranda of agreements, service level agreements, etc.

This is linked to the various project stages and applicable criteria has been developed for each stage.

Project Stakeholder Management

Project Stakeholder Management involves the identification of people, groups or organizations that could impact or be impacted by the project, analysis of their expectations, and the development of effective strategies for engaging stakeholders in project decisions and execution.

In Conclusion

We are Noah and we all have a part to play in preserving endangered animal and plant species while conserving all the other animals and plants not yet endangered.

Planning & Environmental Impact Assessments

Currently, The Noah's Ark Foundation, together with its third party stakeholders are conducting Environmental Impact Assessments (EIA), as well as land assessments, so that Noah's Ark can have a better indication of what biodiversity issues it will face when it comes to construction of the park and stocking the area with wildlife.

But what exactly is an EIA? The Secretariat of the Convention on Biological Diversity, also known as SCBD, explains it very well. EIA is a process of evaluating the likely environmental impacts of a proposed project or development, taking into account inter-related socio-economic, cultural and human-health impacts, both beneficial and detrimental. The UN Environment Programme (UNEP) defines EIA as a tool used to identify the environmental, social and economic impacts of a project prior to decision-making. It aims to predict environmental impacts at an early stage in project planning and design, find ways and means to reduce adverse impacts, shape projects to suit the local environment and present the predictions and options to decision-makers.

By using EIA both environmental and economic benefits can be achieved, such as reduced cost and time of project implementation and design, as well as the avoidance of treatment/clean-up costs and impacts of laws and regulations.

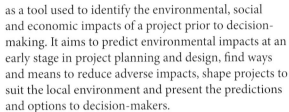

Although legislation and practice vary around the world, the fundamental components of an EIA would necessarily involve the following stages:

a) **Screening** to determine which projects or developments require a full or partial impact assessment study;

b) **Scoping** to identify which potential impacts are relevant to assess (based on legislative requirements, international conventions, expert knowledge and public involvement), to identify alternative solutions that avoid, mitigate or compensate for adverse impacts on biodiversity (including the option of not proceeding with the development, finding alternative designs or sites which avoid the impacts, incorporating safeguards in the design of the project, or providing compensation for adverse impacts), and finally to derive terms of reference for the impact assessment;

c) **Assessment and evaluation of impacts and development of alternatives**, to predict and identify the likely environmental impacts of a proposed project or development, including the detailed elaboration of alternatives;

d) **Reporting the Environmental Impact Statement (EIS) or EIA report,** including an Environmental Management Plan (EMP), and a non technical summary for the general audience;

e) **Review of the Environmental Impact Statement (EIS)**, based on the terms of reference (scoping) and public (including authority) participation;

f) **Decision-making** on whether to approve the project or not, and under what conditions; and

g) **Monitoring, compliance, enforcement and environmental auditing**. Monitor whether the predicted impacts and proposed mitigation measures occur as defined in the EMP. Verify the compliance of proponents with the EMP, to ensure that unpredicted impacts or failed mitigation measures are identified and addressed in a timely fashion.

Figure 138 Climate change on biodiversity (photo: Peta Photography)

The EIA process is quite a lengthy one, looking at the procedures listed from a to g. The world is in a race against time, and usually time always wins. But will we allow that to happen now? Well, that depends on the general population, and governmental input and willingness to help where necessary to speed up the process.

Generally, the process itself takes six months from start to finish in South Africa. Wilbrink & Associates in South Africa explains it beautifully: "The timeframe for an EIA is initially determined by the type of assessment process to be undertaken which will be either Basic Assessment or Full EIA. Generally the Basic Assessment is shorter than the Full EIA because in the Basic Assessment the potential impacts to the environment are already identified and the study revolves around these potential 'knowns' whereas in the Full EIA, the potential still require identification before the study can progress. Ideally the Basic

Assessment Process should take six months while the Full EIA a year but it is never that straight-forward and unforeseeable factors creep up affecting the progress of EIAs. These delays vary with each individual project and in our experience, usually arise during the public participation process."

So this means that The Noah's Ark Foundation should have started with the EIA assessments already because it can take anything from six months to a year. The problem however is that these EIAs are quite costly and, due to the lack of funds for this specific task, Noah's Ark could not have started the process earlier.

However, what the Foundation can do, is to submit a plea to the Department of Environmental Affairs (DEA) in Pretoria, to expedite the process, so that the project can get an outcome on the application sooner rather than later. This however is not where the process ends. Should the application be declined due to certain risk factors, the Foundation can then decide to either move the project to a different location that does not present the specific risk factors, or appeal the application. The appeal of an application could take another six to 12 months, and in itself would be a risk to the project as the Foundation simply does not have the time to waste.

However, the Foundation is rather confident as previous applications for conservation in the same area were submitted and approved by other projects that didn't have the funding to continue. The EIA can be built on the application of previous projects as motivation, notwithstanding that there are already existing conservation facilities in the area.

And then of course there is the land survey. But what exactly is that and what does it entail? Well let's have a look. Land Survey Africa says that: "Land surveying is the science of determining the positions of points, as well as the distances and angles between them, as they are found in a particular geographical area."

Now from my understanding, it is basically mapping out the area you want to build on, where exactly you want to place each building, and that ties into the EIA. Mapping the actual construction will show that and indicate the area of impact on the environment. I might be wrong however, but it just makes sense to me. I mean how else would you know exactly what area will be impacted, to complete an EIA?

So, while The Noah's Ark Foundation is busy conducting the relevant assessments and surveys, we also need to engage with the community and public. That will also play a big part in the EIA process, as seen earlier. Noah's Ark has luckily already started with this task. What we also need to do, as a matter of urgency, is to engage with the Department of Environmental Affairs both in KwaZulu-Natal and the Head Office in Pretoria. That's to expedite the process, so that construction can begin as soon as possible.

Figure 139 Aerial view of Noah's Ark land in KZN ZA

Figure 140 Survey of Noah's Ark land

MANAGEMENT AND SUPPORT

The Team

Richard
Founder, Noah's Ark Foundation

Figure 141 Richard Prinsloo Curson (photo: Monique De Paiva)

Richard grew up with three brothers and two sisters on a rural English farm, went to college to study Media and at 16 had his first book of poetry published Burst with Verse! He went on to broadcast for two years on Magic AM in Yorkshire, then moved to London and under renowned publicist Jules Just learned the craft of making stars out of people and their brands.

Richard Curson the publicist became a familiar face on the London social circuit hosting some of the most memorable celebrity parties in the capital including a series of Club4Climate parties for climate change awareness and worked with the most famous media brands in the country including *OK! Magazine*

and ITV. Richard has worked with familiar faces and brands around the world, helping them make impacts and impressions through what they do in the media. He has assisted in sharing news and views, working with media brands on special assignments, helping produce content for audiences around the world.

Now of course Richard is hard at work on the Noah's Ark project. With so much to do and so little time to waste, Richard is involved in each and every aspect of every project that has to do with Noah's Ark. From fundraising to planning the development. Richard is also busy with the production journey of building a modern day, 21st-century Ark.

Hein
Founder, Noah's Ark Foundation

Figure 142 Hein Prinsloo Curson (photo: Monique De Paiva)

Hein grew up with three brothers, sons of a hard-working South African gold miner and mother Hannatjie Prinsloo, and in search of a better life the family moved from Johannesburg to Pretoria. After matriculation he started a career in Furniture Retail Operations where, having excelled as Regional Operations Manager, he was ready for new dreams to champion.

He met celebrity publicist Richard Curson from London, the two became life partners and eventually had a most beautiful wedding filmed for SABC TV's *Top Billing* show. Hein resigned from retail and the couple launched a Public Relations agency in South Africa. With their respective backgrounds they perfected service delivery for clients by closing the misunderstood gap between Public Relations and Retail. They were ready to take on vast markets. And with the full support of his family, he having come out as gay, there were no more obstacles for this young determined Virgo to accomplish his dreams.

The couple, sharing common goals and aspirations, started expanding their rapidly growing business and flying the SA flag high around the world. Now, working side by side with Richard on the most challenging task of his life, Hein is fully engaged on building the Ark. Running mostly the business side of things (as someone has to) Hein is mostly in charge of making sure that all legalities are sorted, in place, and maintained on a regular basis, while also working on production of the TV series.

Kgaugelo
Noah's Ark Community Project Director

Polica Kgaugelo Sekhwela came from the City of Entity consultant company responsible for community benefit management in Social Housing Projects. As Community Project Director, he is now committed to helping communities integrate into the Noah's Ark project, providing job opportunities, skills training and careers with sustainable incomes far preferable to poaching.

Figure 143 Polica Kgaugelo Sekhwela (photo: Monique De Paiva)

Thobekile Ndlovu ("Thobe") is founder and Managing Director of construction company Thobethulani Trading, and went on to build its reputation as one of the most reliable construction companies in the province (Durban). She has appeared on television and in magazines talking about what it takes to be a female leader in a male-dominated industry. Honoured by KZN Master Builders Association with Best Woman in Construction 2016, then Excellence in Construction 2017, Thobe went on to become an Executive Board Member in 2018. Her first business was in interior design, Impressing Designs, which started trading with a contract from uShaka Marine World. She then won contracts from KwaZulu-Natal legislature and the Department of Trade and Industry.

As Co-Owner of Prinsloo Curson Productions and Noah's Ark Director for KZN she will be providing expert advice to the Noah's Ark project over the next few years, appearing on the television programme to help the team and viewers better understand the construction challenges and solutions involved with the ground-breaking engineering of Noah's Ark.

Thobekile
Noah's Ark Foundation - Director KZN

Figure 144 Thobekile Ndlovu ("Thobe") (photo: Monique De Paiva)

Christina
Noah's Ark Woman's Ambassador & Project leader

Christina Mkhabela is Noah's Ark Woman's Ambassador & Project leader. A personal trainer, model and vocalist, she won various pageants including Miss Soweto and Miss SA Bikini in her teenage years and has recently appeared on SABC TV's *Top Billing* show and The Naledi Theatre Awards broadcast on Kyknet South Africa. As a House music-vocalist she is signed to The Addicted Group Record Company. She joins Noah's Ark to investigate how women will help shape the project and looks at the roles women play now, during the development and when Noah's Ark is open for business.

Figure 145 Christina Mkhabela (photo: Monique De Paiva)

Peta
Noah's Ark Animal Expert

Figure 146 Peta Janice Smith (photo: Monique De Paiva)

Peta Janice Smith came to the project as an overland ranger for a tour operator and is now Noah's Ark Animal Expert. As a child she immersed herself in nature, playing with insects, wild animals and reading books about the natural world around her. She had many funny encounters with nature. Her previous work experience was in Namibia, the Fish River Canyon for the Gondwana Collection, Drifters Adventure centre travelling to nine different African countries living with nature. She joins the Noah's Ark team to travel the animal kingdom worldwide to find species for the Ark; in the process she meets poachers and hunters, talks to experts, and uncovers the stories behind the conservation crisis.

Omee
Noah's Ark Brand Ambassador

Figure 147 Omee Otis (photo: Monique De Paiva)

Now a Noah's Ark Ambassador, Omee is well known for: performing over 70 shows across South Africa; sharing stages with the likes of Cassper Nyovest, Riky Rick, Kwesta, Dj Maphorisa; musical projects with King Monada; performances at the 1st Annual F.A.M.E Ceremony Awards as well as Pretoria's club TOPFLO launch. He was interviewed on SABC 1 by Mzanzi Insider, Touch Central radio, Thobela FM, Radio Turf, GCR. In his musical community talent event H.H.A.T.S, he hosted TV guests Clement Maosa and Cornet Mamabola from soap "Skeem Saam". His School Tour inspired young Limpopo students through motivational speaking, prize giving and performances.

Hannatjie
Noah's Ark Team Manager

Figure 148 Hannatjie Prinsloo (photo: Monique De Paiva)

Since joining her son's business, Prinsloo Curson Productions, Hannatjie Prinsloo as Office and Team Manager is very much the mum of the company, making sure the team is looked after, they have a shoulder to cry on and of course managing the team's busy schedules and activities, ensuring smooth sailing of the Ark's progress so to speak.

Tholoana
Noah's Ark Production Manager

Tholoana Molapo (Tholo) has built a successful career in the broadcasting and entertainment industry over the past 12 years. She can multi-task and has the ability to work on different projects running concurrently due to her in depth experience in the broadcasting industry. She has proven to have the versatility to move from in front of the camera, and on stage to behind the scenes of different productions as production manager, content producer and coordinator to name a few.
She has worked on shows like *Top Billing, Afternoon Express, Pasella, Expresso, 1's and 2's, Code green* etc etc.

Figure 149 Tholoana Molapo (Tholo) (photo: Monique De Paiva)

Brett
Noah's Ark Brand Manager

Figure 150 Brett Rory Lipman (photo: Monique De Paiva)

Brett Rory Lipman is Noah's Ark Brand Manager. He sees himself as a brand director, culture hacker and outsourced professional consultant under the guise of Rebel Africa. Brett is the ultimate people's person and problem solver. Brand development and people management are his passion and he has the ability and foresight to communicate each of his endeavours on a level that is meaningful, intimate and effective.

Javis Talwar 13, of Malaysia,
Global Youth Ambassador, The Noah's Ark Foundation

Javis is a young teenager (13 years old) who loves spending time with nature, exploring and learning about animals where he lives in Malaysia. The countryside is large and ideal for exploring the rain forest, hill stations and tropical islands. He can't stand it when people kill or hunt animals for greed and wants to travel to different countries to experience their way of living, their cultures, their food and to spread awareness about nature and animals. He once suffered 3rd degree burns from spilt coffee, and ever since has felt for animals in pain or that are killed.

NOAH'S ARK **Jeanique**
Singer and Songwriter

Figure 151 Jeanique Danté Fourie
(photos: www.dannychapters.com)

Jeanique Danté Fourie is a young South African singer with a fabulous career ahead of her. Her highlights include: Gold Medals as a soloist in 2016-2018 Talent Africa, Nationals; winning the 2017 International Modelling and Talent Association competition; a duet with Tima Reese; performed with Jonathan Roxmouth; and featured performer in Born to Perform 2018 at Gold Reef Lyric Theatre, Johannesburg.

Monism: the awareness of how little of the world you'll experience.

Whether we think about it or not, our time on this planet is short lived, so it's time we make the most of it. You do only die once...

Instead of living carelessly now, without considering future generations that will inhabit the land we live on, we should live our best lives mindful of what our actions may cause.

Growing up I used to play outside a lot. We lived in a small complex in the suburbs of Johannesburg,

South Africa where everyone knew each other and all the kids would play in the street together, laughing the days away.

The reality of life today is that we are inside almost all of the time. We live in a virtual world where everything is seemingly perfect. However, if the human race keeps living so carelessly, my generation will not be able to live out our elderly years like our parents and grandparents could... and our children will most likely have to fight just to survive.

When I first heard about "Noah's Ark" I thought that their message was so powerful, and I wanted to contribute by sharing this incredible cause with kids my age.

I feel that if we all work together we can help create a future worth looking forward to; a future with blue skies, green grass and animals such as polar bears and rhinos that won't just exist in history books.

In my capacity as Noah, I will be writing and recording a song about world conservation, to remind people that we cannot keep discarding this stunning work of art we live on.

Music has always been a huge part of my life. Ever since I was a young child, nothing could make me feel like a stunning melody could; the execution of the notes, the lyrics sung, the beat, the bass. Music has amazing power to communicate emotion and I would like to share my music with everyone to help bring across this strong message.

I am truly overjoyed to be an ambassador for this project and feel like I've been blessed with an ultra rare opportunity, which I cannot wait to make the most of. I want to create the best song I possibly can, to produce and perform it to the best of my ability.

Art is everywhere around us, in every small detail. Music lives in and around us: in the rain; in the words we speak; in the melodies we hum; the drums we play; the sound of shoes clicking on the pavement; birds chirping; the sound of a mother's heartbeat as she holds her newborn child to her chest. The sound of music is truly to be heard in it all.

Claire
Noah's Ark Public Relations

Figure 152 Claire Barber PR

When The Noah's Ark Team first approached Claire of Claire Barber PR (CBPR), her reaction was astonishing! This is what Claire had to say upon further interviews:

Five years ago I remember seeing a clear-eyed man in a safari outfit on Linkedin. He looked like Bear Grylls and on closer inspection I noted that he was based in South Africa. Something resonated and I instinctively clicked *connect*. Little did I know that the man was Richard Prinsloo Curson and completely out of the blue five years later and 6,000 miles away, he would call me to take on one of the biggest PR projects of my career when he offered CBPR the international PR contract.

Later on he admitted that he had watched my work from afar and was impressed with my 'real' attitude. He related to the mix of PR success stories and glimpses into my life juggling a business and a young family.

"Hi Claire, I hope you are well! Would you be interested in chatting to me about doing the UK PR for Noah's Ark?"

"Hi Richard, would I ever!" I replied.

Having worked with some of the most enviable accounts and high-profile individuals in the UK and on a recent trip to Cannes to cover the film festival, I had been looking for an international account to showcase my PR skills and international contacts. Here was my golden opportunity. And do you know what? I really liked this guy. His attitude, his goals, but especially the thought of contributing in some way to the environment. We had lengthy telephone calls to establish that we could work together and before long I started to engage with Richard's husband Hein. Two such different people but with one, beautiful, goal.

How could I resist the chance to send such an important story to the world's media. Listening to this passion in his voice, pouring his heart out on the plans for the world's most ambitious and technically advanced animal conservation facility, was inspiring. Somehow everything just slotted neatly into place and immediately the plans started to formulate in my brain.

Good Morning Britain, This Morning, Newsnight, Loose Women, the national newspapers, the *New York Times*, the *BBC*, my mind whirring with the endless possibilities for interviews and coverage. That first phone call with *Good Morning Britain* was surreal, "How do you feel about a live with two elephants, a world elephant expert and the founder of Noah's Ark. Did I mention this would be live from the bush in South Africa?". After a huge amount of work and negotiation behind the scenes we pulled off a live broadcast with Charlotte Hawkins and Adil Ray.

It was rather stressful. Try getting a satellite truck into the middle of nowhere, finding accommodation for all the crew and *getting* a decent signal! They say never work with children and animals, but I have yet to have this proved – the majestic elephants Chova and Chisuru stole the show while trying to pinch elephant expert Sean Hensman's hat!

The PR started well with a piece in *The Daily Mail*. It was quickly picked up around the world and we were off … the "live" with GMB was the icing on the cake. At this point we won't mention that it got cancelled then re-booked, argh the stress!

At the same time, Richard, Hein and the Noah's Ark team were filming a documentary and he casually dropped into the conversation that I would form part of the filming for the 13-part documentary and how would I like my company name to appear on the credits, oh and can you write a chapter for the first You Are Noah book? Well, I was on the rollercoaster and we were at the top. Hold on, we're off!

So naturally I am used to being behind the camera, I film a lot of interviews and I am rather bossy (in the name of art) throwing my clients into the deep end. Here I was, like a rabbit in headlights understanding exactly how they felt. Obviously my first thought was "what shall I wear!"

The TV filming was fascinating. Every day Richard and Hein would send behind the scenes images of the animals and crew. Without missing a heartbeat, they would meet the animals without a flicker of fear on their faces. I knew that the world would be fascinated, but it was my huge role to make sure that as many people knew about it as possible prior to broadcast. I mentally felt the world's PR agencies snapping at my heels … This was an enormous project for any PR agency worldwide and it had landed right in my lap. I knew this would be very intensive, but I was ready for it.

My father's favourite statement has always been "you make your own luck in this life" and I do believe this. Going head to head with London agencies I have bagged some pretty A-list clients over the years, earning the reputation as a "clever little PR cookie".

Days filming press calls with news anchors and journalists with The Duchess of Northumberland and her brainchild The Alnwick Garden by Alnwick Castle in the UK and a host of celebrity interviews on TV with golfer Lee Westwood, footballer Alan Shearer and TV duo Ant & Dec have given me incredible experience in my career and of course expanded my little black PR contacts book. I am always mindful that it is just as special to work with a local company just down the road, as it is to work with some of the world's best known celebrities. It's about people.

Deeply heart warming on another level entirely was filming open heart surgery on tiny babies and the Children's Heart Unit as well as raising money for Teenage Cancer and opening accommodation for parents for The Sick Children's Trust whose children were often hundreds of miles away from home. So many varied and thoroughly interesting areas that remind you how precious life is and equally how important it is to enjoy your work. It's true, you never work a day in your life if you love what you do.

So despite being momentarily daunted, nothing is more nerve wracking than mistakenly sending

a text to Anton Du Beke; saying "I love you". Yes I really did! You know, that moment when you press send into the ether and there's nothing you can do to stop it! Of course it was meant for someone else and Anton being Anton, he rang me immediately to tell me "I love you too Claire Barber!". Anton (*Strictly Come Dancing*) is one of the nicest men I have ever met. Handling the PR for one of his dancing tours, he wrote "I love you Claire Barber" in my programme after the show one night.

"Good evening Claire, we need to find a clothing sponsor for our team, can you help?"

Enter Liz Jackson. Her nickname is Glammy. Editor of one of the most exclusive glossy magazines, long blonde hair and after years working together, now one of my best friends. I facetime her sitting in bed in my PJs at 5am UK time. Wild hair, no make-up. She doesn't bat an eyelid, sitting at her kitchen table surrounded by fabric swatches, magazines and her usual coffee.

"I need your help. You won't believe the account I am working on".

I WhatsApp over the video of Noah's Ark and give her the gen on the project. We have that shorthand understanding that only comes with years of friendship and light years working together. She gets it immediately.

Typical Liz, she takes it a step further. A former alumnus of the prestigious London College of Fashion, she has covered the catwalks of London Fashion Week and worked with almost all the high street and designer brands. She's interviewed everyone in the industry from the editor of *Vogue* to Zandra Rhodes. Her favourite cocktail is a Mimosa and we may have had one or two over the years!

"I know exactly who we need to speak to, but I will only take this on if I can style everyone".

Relief washes over me. I know Richard will love this. Now what's next on my list …

"Good morning Claire, the plans include an airstrip. We will need to transport animals and different species from around the world. We've just been discussing transport for polar bears this morning with the vets".

I am just waiting to hear the words "can you organise an airline to sponsor Noah's Ark?" They don't come … yet.

I go to bed thinking about Noah's Ark. I'm dreaming about huge polar bears asking for in-flight service. I wake up, drink coffee, add to the next day's lists and open my phone to behind the scenes filming, images and videos of hippos, zebras and snakes from Richard. This is so surreal and all encompassing.

Our daily calls are peppered with the sounds of squawking wild parrots and what Richard describes as "dinosaur birds". Huge black, long beaked Hadidas birds that interrupt our calls with their chatter. We divert from our conversations with stories of snakes and deadly spiders making their way into his home which he shares with husband Hein. I've made it very clear that I am terrified of spiders and would prefer to come face to face with a rhino. All of a sudden we are friends as well as work colleagues. Today's story is about finding a large spider on Richard's herb collection on the kitchen windowsill. He sends a photograph to one of his vets who tells him to to remove it from the house immediately or there will be millions, yes millions, of baby spiders invading his home. The offer to come and stay becomes less palatable, yet still I pinch myself.

Photographs and videos fill my timeline as I build my own view and start to get to know this passionately focused man.

"Good morning Claire. I am planning ocean-based team building with dolphins, whales and possibly sharks, can you help with a contact?".

Never before have I wanted so much to be part of a team-building exercise. I love the ocean and everything to do with water and boats.

"Good morning Claire. Can I ask you a really, really big favour? Like huge?"

I simply cannot predict what Richard and I will discuss. Of course, I say yes. I'm 100%, wholeheartedly in, even though I literally have no idea what he is going to say.

I flick open my contact book. "Investors and philanthropists invited to acquire shares". Even though this is not strictly PR, I run my finger down the list and set about texting a line or two. We are talking billions here. Billions to save our animals. It's a small price in the big scheme and I realise that I am a tiny part in the vastness of Noah's Ark." – Claire Barber

Claire Barber is the CEO of Claire Barber PR Ltd

Social Media Influence

Social Media Consultant, Mariska Van Eeden, Explains Why she Joined the Noah's Ark Project

Figure 153 Mariska Van Eeden, Eeden Social Media Marketing

One's life can be brought to a halt, in a few key moments. When one takes a first step, utters a first word, or truly realises being part of this world. However only a fortunate few can truly grasp what existence really is. I was young and once had a remarkable obsession with our solar system. Unmeasurable space expanding the borders of what we humans used to believe was our world.

This all changed when my parents took me to see the mountain ranges for the first time. The vast chasms expanding, much like space, infinitely as far as the eye can see. My mind was used to the idea that the Earth was small, and like many young people today, I believed our salvation lay in the stars. My father was no man of science, he had the gift of taking in the 'now', and believed beauty was all around us, if we only took a moment to take it in. He was so excited in showing

us the glory of the sea, I wasn't convinced at the time. It couldn't be that big could it?

I was lost for words when I first heard the waves in the distance, huge hills formed only from salty liquid. The crashes seemed even more intense, given my young age. To those who grew up on the coastline it was just another day, yet to someone like me it was a whole new world that just popped up and came to be. Beaches that stretched down as far as the eye can see, rivalled only by the big blue giant. The flat blue phenomenon seemed endless; my eyes tried to make out the other side but to no avail. I had so many questions: What's on the other side; why do the waves crash and get back up; why is it even there? I was lost in a world of mystery, and wanted answers.

My grandparents loved nature, numerous times I would find my grandfather simply sitting and admiring the coloured bark on the trees. I found it odd at the time, simply because I was too young to fully appreciate the wonders mother nature gives us. My curiosity was finally met when my grandparents took me to the Cape Town Aquarium for the first time. I not only learned more about the ocean, but I had found a whole underwater kingdom. Numerous different tribes, each special in their very own way. Fish who prefer schools to help better protect themselves from predators; rays, who glide like aeroplanes slightly above the ocean floor; octopi, who could instantly camouflage between rocks; and crustaceans with their bug like, exoskeleton bodies. But of course, like any youngster, I was more preoccupied with the carnivorous sharks. Only much later, would I come to realise the significance of all sea creatures, and the ecosystem they form when they're together.

The age of connectivity had come to fruition, and I had tried to learn all my parents were willing to teach me. Never before was the knowledge of the world at our fingertips, it was alluring, like a drug. I became lost in information, all the questions about existence could finally be answered by those who had studied it for generations. This ecstasy was suddenly halted, when I learned that we had barely scratched the surface of the blue giant, when it came to discovery. More than 80% of the big blue is unmapped, and who knows what beauty there is just waiting to be found. My curiosity was unsated, but I had grown up since I was a young individual. I realised why my grandfather enjoyed the coloured bark on the trees, and why we all stop now and then to smell the flowers. The world wasn't beautiful because it gave us answers, what made it beautiful is how everything we see in nature is doing its fair share. There is no gluttony or greed among the fish in the sea, there is no separatism among the children of nature. They've continued to thrive, now even in these polluting times. Why? Because they live and let live.

Why can we not do the same? Humanity has always indulged in the resources and the beauty of nature while still preserving her. What changed, we are all still the children of our ancestors who gave their respects to the earth which provided for them? Yet selfish greed has led us astray, we have abandoned the principles those before had set for us, in search of new-found wealth. True wealth is experiencing this world the way it was always meant to be experienced. Not through

images of what once was. We simply need hope, for hope is what causes us to push and carry on even when the odds are stacked against us. Alone we can surely not make a difference, but if we stand together – we can overcome any obstacle standing between us and the beauty of all the Earth's children. Some of us gave up a long time ago, including myself, but then I became aware of the Noah's Ark organisation. Seeing their commitment to ensuring the survival of countless creatures of the earth reignited my faith. If they had the courage to push onward even when they had plenty of reasons not to, why could I not. The time is nigh, to stand up and give back what was taken and restore the symbiotic balance between humanity and nature.

Not too long ago, a friend of mine came to me and told me with wonder in his eyes that a rhino was actually a large creature. I was confused because of course it was. Only after a few moments later, I realised they and countless other animals were on the verge of extinction. And that some people may never see those creatures in person again, as some never have; a privilege I had enjoyed would be stripped from the younger generation.

The Noah's Ark conservation stepped forth to ensure our youngling of the future get to experience what I had experienced as a youth. Starting construction of the world's largest-scale aquarium would ensure that the dream of conservation would come to fruition. It would provide a ray of combined hope, shining down on countless generations to come; proving to those who had lost hope, that we just need to keep pushing forward. The massive Ark project would house countless sea life species, where those who are both familiar and unfamiliar can grasp the Earth's beauty once again. A place where future marine biologists would make their career choice; a place where the children watch the dolphins play; while those with the love of music, can take a quiet step and listen to the ancient sound of the whales singing.

Children do not experience sea life as a myth that once was, but a beautiful reality

Noah's Ark truly represents a realm of new possibilities, and so as they are new, so are they endless. Following them in their march to a better life for all the Earth's children, I have discovered that my dream of a beautiful symbiotic world has returned. A world where we all can live in perfect harmony. A world where those who were once lost in man-made cities, oblivious to dying nature around them, can finally see what they've been missing, and see that they have the ability not only to help create this sea life paradise for those in need, but they have the ability to change the future. This will mean their children do not experience sea life as a myth that once was, but a beautiful reality that is.

I, like many others, do not fear the extinction of wild and sea life, I'm older now and most questions that I had have been answered. I was fortunate enough to witness their existence myself. And, like most, I regularly ask myself: is a fight like this even worth fighting for? If the time and effort I put into anything else, is better for my personal wellbeing. And if I had to ask myself that question it would be: no. But if that's the way we approached mankind we would have been extinct a long time ago. In the end, we all know our time is limited. It might be something some of us catch on to too late, when we truly realise it's not what we take with us that matters. What matters is what we leave behind. It's why we try to teach others; it's why we show compassion; it's why we take in injured or abused animals; and it's why we seek a loved one to build a family with.

We all leave something behind as an example for those who come after. Most of us have seen most animals, but those who come after us might not. What will we decide to leave for them? A trail of hope, prosperity and dedication to boost their confidence for a better tomorrow? A society working together, to achieve something greater than they ever expected? Or will we leave a path of greed, gluttony, destruction and disdain. Only proving to them there is no hope for change?

Not sit idly by as the great and beautiful world I grew up in crumbles and erodes

Something we all share is destiny, and unlike in the movies, ours is not certain. Every choice we make will influence how we will be remembered. And that is why even though my actions are not in the best interest of my personal wellbeing. I will not sit idly by as the great and beautiful world I grew up in crumbles and erodes, so the youth of tomorrow never experiences the true beauty nature has to offer. That is why I've chosen to support Noah's Ark in all their selfless endeavours.

They strive for a future where nature isn't a lost beautiful memory our grandkids will read about in bunkers sheltering themselves from the solar rays that have pierced our damaged atmosphere. But for a future where they will see the beauty first-hand as hope showers their dreams with what is still to come.

Health & Support for The Noah's Ark Team

Mental Health of The Project Managers

Dr Arthur Cassidy Ph.D C.Psychol
Consultant Psychologist to Noah's Ark Project

Figure 154 Dr Arthur Cassidy Ph.D C.Psychol
(photo: Danny Chapters)

Introduction

In this chapter I wish to take you on a journey through the mindset of Richard Prinsloo Curson, President of The Noah's Ark Foundation and Hein Prinsloo Curson, Vice President, as they meet the unforeseen and overwhelming psychological challenges of the world's largest wildlife conservation project. What type of mindset is imperative in the design and overall management of such a phenomenal global concept?

We are all faced with individual and collective traumas, adversity, relationship crises, work problems and have to endure health anxieties such as the worldwide coronavirus and our own psychological vulnerability. During our lifespan we face many hurdles, unwanted and unexpected stresses and have the adaptability to perform quick turnarounds without compromising our mental health. Each crisis at work brings our specific personality types and traits into action and these involve our emotional regulation and cognitive functioning, as well as how we make decisions.

Emotional Resilience

Psychologists worldwide define resilience as the process of adapting efficiently and maintaining psychological control in the face of adversity tragedy, self-perceived threats such as completion of the Noah's Ark project on time, and successful management of people and co-workers. In addition, their emotional resilience could be jeopardized as the project grows in capacity with the building of various GeoDomes, landscaping, legalities, and the entire infrastructure. Self-doubt may set in along the journey, besides financial stressors, so the project requires psychological expertise at a high level in diagnosing the stress triggers early on and coaching the founders into high levels of performance with professional psychological interventions such as Solution Focused Brief Therapy, Mindfulness sessions and Cognitive Behavioural Therapy. While Richard and Hein face continuous challenges, many profoundly adverse, these don't have to direct and control their life. Learning the art of empowerment through the development of a resilient mind gets things done and maximises self-perceived competences.

Build positive networks with positive successful people

It's vital to build positive networks with positive successful people who matter and who can empathise with you. Psychological health and wellbeing involves dedication and commitment to achieving SMART goals and taking care of self.

I have also planned a three-month course of action for Richard and Hein in personal fitness in order to overcome stress anxiety and help them have a clear focus on prioritising events and having sufficient mental and physical stamina to endure the long journey ahead. Now these guys are involved with Planet Fitness in regular high intensity workouts that I have built into their sessions with me.

Other obstacles could be thinking too far ahead which can overwhelm oneself with fear and negativity. Working together, my task is to help them restructure how they have been thinking in the past and how they can now modify their irrational thinking and replace this with lots of smaller achievements week by week and month by month. It's all about Mindfulness techniques and living in the present. This technique is extremely useful in only paying attention to what's happening now, letting go of all the worries about the future and learning new relaxation and breathing techniques and their management. Our working together has a focus on accepting change and circumstances that are not beneficial to our mental health and reorienting our motives into achieving other strategies that maximise positive outcomes. It's about engaging with courage and fortitude and developing attitudes of stoicism along the way.

Personalities of the Team

When I first had a conversation with Richard and Hein just before the end of 2020, it became clear that they were experiencing profound psychological distress, anguish and panic with bouts of depression and anxiety. It was obvious that the vision they both had of creating a modern-day Noah's Ark fit for purpose for centuries to come, would be imbued with technological scientific and environmental complexities and major stressors beyond their control, in securing the right level of investment to the tune of £5 billion ($7 billion), and much more. In addition, the extraordinary size of this international conservation project made it mandatory to employ a range of project managers whose brief was to understand with clarity what their specific roles and functions were and how they would meet their targets and deadlines, demonstrating their range of skills and competences and working as competent and effective team members.

At its beginning it would have been impossible to fully comprehend the intricacies and human complexities in managing various multicultural identities in the project team with various degrees of potential intercultural conflict over decision making and achievement of project aims and goals. Individual personalities with their own invariably changing social perceptions of the project, are anchored deep in their own attitudes and beliefs which could be psychologically destructive to the overall project, if not identified and managed effectively early on in team planning and coordination. In such a phenomenally global project, major and minor stressors like these are central to the daily workload of human resource management.

Television and Social Media

Noah's Ark Project has added major stress variables as it is one of the world's largest ever media events to take place on the world stage. The project has become very much newsworthy outside daily news broadcasts on COVID-19 with soaring death rates, and international politics; each day we hear bad news and few good news stories. This is a huge and colourful story on planet earth at the moment and will be for years to come. We ask the question why is it newsworthy? Recently the high-profile ITV breakfast show Good Morning Britain gave the Noah's Ark project well received air time and coverage, with informative interviews about the endangered species in South Africa and around the world. It was a sheer joy to see the interviews with Richard and the elephant expert, besides Hein and other project experts in other high-profile interviews.

Television has the capacity to influence our emotional functioning and attitude formation, more so at this time when the world needs to listen to positive world events which can induce positive mood states and help us move from pessimism to optimism. The intensity of the stressors became more dominant when the project became a major television series produced by Globetrotter Television in the UK. As a celebrity and social media TV psychologist for many years and one who spends time with TV journalists almost weekly, I know at first hand the psychological stress and anxiety involved in being media ready for specialist television interviews. There is the preparation of media content with your PR for prime time TV coverage and exposure on the global market. It's about getting the story right and having to negotiate with producers on what to leave in – and out. What do viewers need to know, and how they present themselves and their image on high-profile television programmes. With constant media exposure and global broadcasting networks requesting interviews, Richard and Hein have to deal with the anxiety of reorganising business meetings and other daily events. The anxiety moves from one-off acute episodes to chronic stress and anxiety. When heading up such a world event the global media exposure brings with it a moral obligation to deliver the project on target. This in itself is a hugely stressful life experience and requires psychological interventions and prolonged support until completion of the Noah's Ark conservation project and beyond.

Children growing up in concrete cities show cognitive deficits in their paucity of knowledge of the animal kingdom and rural development

It is dichotomous in that it presents us with a social conscience trigger – both individually and collectively – on the deliberate destruction of planet Earth and the animal kingdom, by our attitudes and behaviour. It's time for a moral conscience reality check. We have

become so obsessively selfish with ourselves and our focus on urbanisation, we have perpetually ignored the immense value of the countryside and especially the life of the animal kingdom and endangered species. Current scholarly research in developmental psychology has provided objective evidence that, with some exceptions, children growing up in concrete cities show cognitive deficits in their paucity of knowledge of the animal kingdom and rural development. Innately humans are created and designed to interact with the animal species and acquire detailed knowledge of their social and rearing behaviours. It's imperative that we become more introspective and be mindful of our need to care for and protect our beloved animal kingdom and its natural habitat.

Urban environments may heighten the risk of psychosis and other mental health issues such as depression and anxiety

An article published in *Scientific American* by Diana Kwon (20th May 2016) points out that "According to a recent U.N. report, the proportion of people living in cities will rise from 54% of the world's population in 2014 to 66% by 2050. Furthermore, she reports that:

"Researchers first suggested in the 1930s that urban living might increase schizophrenia risk. Since then many large epidemiological studies have reported an association between the two, primarily in European countries such as Sweden and Denmark. Converging evidence has revealed that growing up in the city doubles the risk of developing psychosis later in life. Studies have also begun to find that urban environments may heighten the risk of other mental health issues such as depression and anxiety."

Our global self-obsessed selfishness and perpetual destruction of planet Earth by our own hand anchored in our avaricious and covetous attitudes driven by selfish motives and greed for self, is a gross betrayal of our planet and all living creatures and their welfare.

Stress and Coping

Psychologists study objectively and scientifically all aspects of human and animal behaviour and what specific environmental and biological stressors negatively influence their health and wellbeing. These are the stimuli that exert ongoing pressures on our cognitive processes and decision making, as in the Noah's Ark project. At the outset, Richard and Hein had a vision as described in this book, and would have felt socially motivated to achieve their dream. This is a perfectly reasonable, however it invariably comes with totally unforeseen and unexpected psychological costs. These stressors raise the issue as to how these two founders of Noah's Ark can maximise their emotional resilience and their coping skills on a day-to-day basis. My role as the psychologist is to help them identify the triggers of stress and anxiety (the most salient previously described) and to eradicate them or at the very least control them with effective stress management techniques and low intensity cognitive behavioural therapy.   A very common stress-related problem they may have to deal with is in individual members of the team not being effective team members. When one member doesn't demonstrate their commitment to the team leader it's called 'Social Loafing'. In this scenario the individual concerned either loses interest in his or her contribution or the project aims and objectives overall. Other issues they have and will continue to face are coping with the physical stressors. Early mornings, late nights, insomnia, appetite loss, and fatigue set in and are health warnings to calm down and keep things in perspective. Delegation is vital in the overall management of a mammoth wildlife and conservation project, so is organisation and structures. This is where we have to release the stress and anxiety triggers and ensure that other project managers are fully competent to ensure goals and deadlines are met on time. In summary let us all become Noahs individually and collectively and save our planet Earth and the animal kingdom.

Figure 155
Planet Fitness

THE SUPERHERO BODY TRANSFORMATION CHALLENGE

planetfitness

Intrepid Planet Fitness ambassadors, Hein and Richard are pulling together to ring in some seriously ambitious and positive transformations – not only for the conservation of the planet – but for their personal, physical and mental wellbeing as prescribed by Celebrity Psychologist Dr Arthur Cassidy.

Figure 156
Richard & Hein Prinsloo Curson with club manager Sean Maskell

Saving the world starts with saving yourself, so by getting leaner and being health wise you can be Noah too **#youarenoah** and make your small contribution every day. By reducing your body weight you can reduce your personal carbon footprint and boost your quality of life!

Starting the "Superhero Challenge" with Planet Fitness and Ultimate Sports Nutrition (USN), Richard was over 95kg with a target weight of 84kg. By stripping off fat Richard will not only look leaner and meaner (be strong enough to build Noah's Ark) but will be less of a burden on the

world around him because his body weight will need less carbon to keep him going!

In planes or cars Richard's extra unnecessary weight currently means using more fuel. And because his weight was due to excess eating he would consume more food and produce more waste than if he was living a balanced lifestyle with regular exercise.

Food production and logistics together with waste management contribute to carbon emissions, so the more food we eat the more carbon we produce to process it, move it to retail space and cook it at home. The

more food we eat the more packaging we throw away, which means waste processing and more carbon emissions. His excess weight would therefore be contributing unnecessarily to carbon in the atmosphere which is causing global warming.

It's a positive thought that just by looking and feeling good we can be less of a burden on our planet. Imagine if everyone joined Richard to be superheroes at Planet Fitness with Ultimate Sports Nutrition (USN) and what a carbon saving we would collectively make by reaching our ideal body weight!

125

THE NEW SUPERHERO BODY TRANSFORMATION CHALLENGE

Richard and Hein are joined by Kgaugelo and their NEW Personal Trainer Rosana Dos Santos as Fit24Gyms Ambassadors for the intensive strength and shape challenge to support their personal, physical and mental well being as prescribed by Celebrity Psychologist Dr. Arthur Cassidy.

Richard and Hein took on a 3 month fitness challenge to shape up both physically and mentally at the start of 2021. Richard originally weighed 95kg, smashed his body weight target of 84kg and has achieved an impressive 83kg current body weight as of July 2021! And with South Africa zoned as the focal point for the largest and most ambitious conservation project in history, what better place for the Noah's Ark team to progress the fitness challenge than the dynamic Fit24Gyms to build the necessary physical and mental stamina to take on the world. They will be training at the Premier club located inside the 5 star Radisson Blu Hotel Sandton, Rivonia Rd & Daisy St, Sandton, South Africa.

Preserving life on the planet starts with YOU!

Figure 157 Richard Prinsloo Curson working out at Fit24Gyms
All photographs at Fit24Gyms by nick@nickboulton.com

Hein and Richard's Vision of vast 30-storey GeoDomes and the largest aquarium in the world in the form of a state-of-the-art animal and ecological conservation park needs truly superhuman stamina to realise. Raising funds, networking and gathering followers is a round the clock effort. It was no surprise that working day and night for months left them drained. "Feeling unfit was hampering our efforts to keep up the zest required to drive forward at top speed," said Hein. UK celebrity and TV psychologist, Dr Arthur Cassidy, who provides mental health care for the Noah's Ark team advised Richard and Hein to stay healthy throughout this project while the pair film much of their Noah's Ark TV docuseries in South Africa. That's where Fit24Gyms SA jumped in to take the conservationists through their advanced challenge where the goals are strength and muscle definition! By going to the gym several times a week, the pair have already reported feeling more energetic, although they have kept us in stitches with some of their antics on Twitter @Noahsarklife.

That said Richard and Hein are an example of the strength of the human spirit to take on one of the world's most serious challenges.

According to Mayo Clinic, exercise releases endorphins (chemicals in your brain that revitalise your mind and body), reduces negative effects of stress, improves your mood, and can also strengthen your immune system, something that is particularly important for us all right now.

The pair took on a three-month fitness challenge to shape up both physically and mentally at the start of 2021. And, with South Africa zoned as the focal point for the largest and most ambitious conservation project in history, what better place for the Noah's Ark team to buddy up with South Africa's largest, homegrown health and fitness brand, Fit24Gyms to build the necessary physical and mental stamina to take on the world.

Preserving life on the planet starts with YOU

Hein and Richard's vision of vast 30-storey GeoDomes and the largest aquarium in the world in the form of a state-of-the-art animal and ecological conservation park needs truly superhuman stamina to realise. Raising funds, networking and gathering followers is a round-the-clock effort. It was no surprise that working day and night for months left them drained. "Feeling unfit was hampering our efforts to keep up the zest required to drive forward at top speed," said Hein.

UK celebrity and TV psychologist, Dr Arthur Cassidy, who provides mental health care for the Noah's Ark team advised Richard and Hein to stay healthy throughout this project while the pair film much of their Noah's Ark TV docuseries in South Africa. That's where Fit24Gyms jumped in to take the conservationists through their paces with a Fit24Gyms personal trainer who is helping to bring their three-month fitness challenge to life. By going to the gym several times a week, the pair have already reported feeling far more energetic, although they have kept us in stitches with some of their antics on Twitter @Noahsarklife.

That said, Hein and Richard are an example of the strength of the human spirit to take on one of the world's most serious challenges.

According to Mayo Clinic, exercise releases endorphins (chemicals in your brain that revitalise your mind and body), reduces negative effects of stress, improves your mood, and can also strengthen your immune system, something that is particularly important for all of us right now.

Figure 159 Kgaugelo at Fit24Gyms

"It's simple, each one of us on this planet needs to look after our own physical and mental wellbeing as the first stop, particularly in the extraordinary times we are living in."

Figure 160 Hein Prinsloo Curson at Fit24Gyms

Figure 161 Rosanna at Fit24Gyms

Figure 162
Richard Prinsloo
Curson at Fit24Gyms

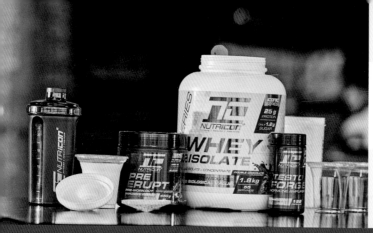

You Are What You Eat

A fitness challenge to build a body to serve a purpose is undoubtedly the most exciting because there is a reason for all the effort, sacrifice and struggle. Changing your lifestyle with a new eating plan and exercise regime is not easy, so NUTRICON provide support, making lifestyle changes a "walk in the park".

"When we heard about the ambitious Noah's Ark project we knew founders Richard and Hein had their work cut out and from a wellbeing perspective and needed to further prime their bodies to cope with the ever increasing tremendous pressures managing a project of this scale brings. They have already succeeded because they have generated positive global coverage highlighting important ecological issues but we wanted to

help them go even further!" said a NUTRICON spokesperson.

Richard and Hein will be joined by the Noah's Ark Communities Director Polica Kgaugelo Sekhwela (a.k.a. Kgaugelo) and Rosana Dos Santos who is their personal trainer for the NEW Superhero Body Transformation challenge. Alongside Fit24Gyms personal training programme Richard, Hein, and Kgaugelo have been given a new eating plan by NUTRICON. For Richard who is now defining muscle, a low fat high protein diet will be followed. Hein is now increasing his carbohydrates to bulk and build. Kgaugelo will be following the same KETO diet Richard and Hein strictly adhered to in the first fitness challenge.

There are 4 main elements to the supplement package. These are:

1	Activate
2	Maximise
3	Fuel
4	Support

Figure 165
Richard and Hein
Prinsloo Curson &
NUTRICON products
(2 photos)

Figure 166
NUTRICON

The four NUTRICON supplements help to support the 3 diet plans in this challenge, making living with the eating plans easy.

Figure 167
NUTRICON

We talked to Richard and Hein to find out more about the challenge and how they are finding the NUTRICON eating plan.

Why did you decide to take on a Superhero challenge?
Richard: After filming and watching myself back on camera, I realised how fat I was getting. I'm not much of a role model when we are trying to inspire people to follow us and believe in us.
Hein: Before NUTRICON we both complained about being tired, bloated and needing a boost! When the challenge was suggested to us, we grabbed it with both hands!

When did you find the USN supplements most beneficial?
Richard: The Fat burners supressed my appetite, so I ate less. And the BHB Salts were my "Go To" supplement when my energy dived during the day.
Hein: For me the MCT oil because I felt fuller for longer. And it motivated my bowel movement so quickly, it debloats and makes you feel better.

What was NUTRICON flu like for you?
Richard: Headache, feeling nauseous, fatigue.
Hein: Very tired, with a headache. And generally feeling down for two days.

Have you discovered new foods you now love through the NUTRICON eating plan?
Richard: Spices and dressings make the blandest of food zesty and delicious!
Hein: Sunflower seeds give a whole new experience to the dullest salad!

What is the hardest part of NUTRICON?
Richard: The first two weeks we had NUTRICON flu, withdrawal symptoms from bad food we liked.
Hein: After the first two weeks it got much easier! Now we are regulating our food intake very well!

What motivates you to succeed with the eating plan?
Richard: Since we started, I have incredible energy and am 100% more productive on the project. This is a superhero challenge, because we effectively need to be superheroes to make this major project happen.
Hein: Also being in the spotlight definitely makes us feel self-conscious, so looking our best makes us perform our best! I can't wait to fit into my favourite shirt again!

Figure 168 NUTRICON

Figure 169 NUTRICON

A new and exciting lifestyle, is the one change anyone anywhere can make to their lives. And after COVID-19 lockdowns around the world, many will be ready to make the most of life and their bodies. The new-found way of life can also impact on the environment; because if we feel good about ourselves we also want to feel good about the world around us!

HERE ARE 3 EASY SWAPS TO HELP YOU STAY FIT AND SAVE THE PLANET AT THE SAME TIME!

BURN FAT! – WALK OR CYCLE

Driving in an SUV for just one mile, adds 1.5 pounds of carbon dioxide to the environment. Walking and cycling not only help to shape up your body and improve fitness, that way you also reduce the harmful greenhouse gases put into the atmosphere. Cycling 6 miles per hour can burn 240 calories! Walking 2 to 3 miles per hour can burn up to 300 calories!

Figure 170
NUTRICON

STAY HYDRATED! – RE USE YOUR BOTTLE

It's essential we stay hydrated to sustain a healthy lifestyle, especially with the NUTRICON eating plan. However, reports of unwanted chemicals in bottled water raised fears about drinking water from disposable plastic bottles. Buying bottled water is a "ridiculous use of plastic and an incredible waste of money," says Trask. Re use your NUTRICON bottles instead of buying bottled water.

EAT FRESH! – LOCALLY SOURCED ORGANIC FOOD

Fruits and vegetables are widely shipped from around the world, which means they are not fresh and lack essential nutrition. So, change your habits and buy local, to get super fresh produce and get the best nutrition from what you eat! Organic food is the best, as it is free of pesticides or other chemicals that are harmful to the planet and your health!

Figure 171 NUTRICON

Figure 172 NUTRICON (2 photos)

South Africa
Corporate Support
SMG Umhlanga

The World of BMW

The area in KwaZulu-Natal where Noah's Ark will be built, is generally hilly and mountainous, especially along the western border of the province.

The land rises from the coast to more than 11,000 feet (3,300 metres) along the Drakensberg Escarpment on that border. The slope is not gradual, however, and various rocky outcrops render the terrain into steps of undulating land ascending from an elevation of 500 feet (150 metres) along the coastal plain to areas of 2,000 feet (600 metres) and then 4,000 feet (1,200 metres) in the centre of the province, a region known as the Midlands. Beyond the Drakensberg lies the Highveld, or high plateau.

To get to the location of Noah's Ark is challenging to say the least, and one does need an off-road vehicle to reach it. Unfortunately for the Noah's Ark team, they needed some help to get to the site for them to do their very important work in the community.

It came as no surprise that SMG picked up the challenge when The Noah's Ark Team went knocking for assistance in off-road vehicles for 4 days. SMG is a privately owned group of Automotive Retail Businesses comprising of Toyota, BMW, MINI, Jaguar and Land Rover. SMG has made a great shift within their dealerships towards achieving their long-term vision and mission of environmental sustainability.

Figure 173 Richard with an SMG Umhlanga BMW on the Noah's Ark project

Their assistance enabled the team to visit the poorest community in KZN, where they met up with an elderly woman who lost her house in a fire, as well a school where they met with teachers and got first hand experience of the working conditions and challenges. Of course they had some fun with the children whilst there. All of this can be seen in the Noah's Ark TV show as it was documented.

SMG really came through and saved the day for the team on this one. As beautiful as the land and the area is in KZN, the rural areas are not the easiest to get to but it most certainly is worth it once you reach the lush beautiful surroundings.

Figure 174 SMG Umhlanga's state BMW dealership

The Umhlanga Arch is home to SMG Umhlanga's state of the art BMW dealership. Sean McCarthy, Managing Director of SMG, says it has always been their goal to provide customers with an 'incredible experience'. "Whether a customer is purchasing a vehicle or requires aftersales assistance, our ethos has always been to maintain a customer centric approach. The Umhlanga Arch development offers our brand a space that provides an unprecedented feeling of awe, aspiration and a design that is undoubtedly trend setting."

The design, layout and flow, makes for an industry leading dealership experience. SMG Umhlanga has many unique features, specifically designed and included to offer a BMW lifestyle that takes premium motoring to new heights.

Enjoy the world of BMW at the all new and exciting SMG Umhlanga.

The Galaxy Space Forest Lodge

"Home Away From Home"

Where The Noah's Ark Team Stay in KwaZulu-Natal, South Africa

The Galaxy Forest Lodge, situated in the Thandizwe area in uMhlabuyalingana local Municipality, is a hidden gem privately tucked in at Manguzi sand Forest in the heart of Northern KwaZulu-Natal. The Lodge is 25km away from the Kosi Bay Border to Mozambique, and 43km away from Ponta Dora and Maputo, which is accessible even with a sedan. The Lodge is also 160km away from the Golela Border, thus making it a gateway to Swaziland. Simply put, you can easily have breakfast in Galaxy Forest, lunch in Mozambique and dinner in Swaziland all in one day. Finally the Galaxy Forest Lodge is in close proximity to iSimangaliso Wetland Park Authority jewels (Kosi Mouth, Bhanganek and Sodwana) as well as the Big Five Tembe Elephant Park.

Figure 175 The Galaxy Forest Lodge reception

Figure 176 Forest Lodge bedroom

Figure 177 Forest Lodge bar

Galaxy Forest Lodge offers luxuriously modern self-catering rooms. Fully equipped standard, Executive and family rooms are all designed to guarantee maximum comfort and hospitality from the moment you arrive. All the rooms are equipped with satellite channels, fridge, microwave, air conditioning and telephone. The lodge is mostly roofed with thatch, bringing back the traditional experience in a modern way. It includes outdoor swimming pools, bar and restaurant and conference facilities.

The bar and restaurant is opened for all day dining with a variety of meals to choose from including our famous pizza. All this can be done whilst enjoying the free Wi-Fi provided. It also includes a private lounge with its own private pool and braai area for those who love tranquillity. The private lounge also serves a variety of delicious halal foods.

Figure 178 Forest Lodge reception

Figure 179 Forest Lodge cabins

Figure 180 Forest Lodge swimming pools (2 photos)

The Lodge is child friendly as we provide a Jungle Jim and Trampoline for kids to enjoy playing different games while their parents watch them from the restaurant deck. It also has a small swimming pool suitable for kids.

The Lodge is equipped with a beauty spa with a wide variety of massages, facials, skin care and exclusive treatments to leave you feeling replenished and nurtured. Nothing beats the sounds of various bird species and the roaring sound of the perennial Masulumane stream water constantly flowing to fill up the amazing Kosi Bay lake system, whilst you enjoy a peaceful massage.

Figure 181 Forest Lodge safari ride

Figure 182 Forest Lodge safari ride (2 photos)

The Galaxy Forest Lodge has a variety of activities that guests can enjoy, ranging from quad bikes, Game drives to Tembe Elephant Park (a big five game reserve), Ndumo Game Reserve (known for its exclusive birding), a boat cruise to the three lakes of Kosi Bay which has the freshest lake system on the continent.

If you love nature and outdoor activities, Galaxy Forest Lodge is definitely the place to be. You don't want to miss this wonderful experience, so please do come through and visit us. We can't wait to meet you.

For more information, visit our website on www.thegalaxyspace.co.za or our Facebook page at The Galaxy Lodge.

Figure 183 Forest Lodge quad biking (2 photos)

Illustrations

References

frontiers in Conservation Science, Jan 2021. p4, 6, 7, 8, 9, 10, 19

The Guardian 2018. p5, 12

Science News 2020. p11, 20

U.N. Intergovernmental Science-Policy Platform on Biodiversity and Ecosystem Services 2019 p13, 18

Time – U.N. Environment Programme World Conservation Monitoring Centre. p14

The Guardian – UN on the state of nature 2020 p15

IUCN, official advisory body on nature under the World Heritage Convention p16, 17

Climate Action Summit 2019: A Race We Can Win. A Race We Must Win p21

Plants & Us (date of publication: late 2021) p62

USA Science & Engineering Festival p65

Oceana (8 June 2020) p65

BBC News (7 December 2019) p65

National Ocean Service, National Oceanic and Atmospheric Services, US Department of Commerce p65

NASA, Space Colonisation p74

Big Think (12 July 2019) p74

DeepStorm OutTack (2012) p75

You Ask Andy, When Did Wildlife Conservation Start
p77

Sky News, Climate change: Seven technology solutions
that could help solve crisis p90

en.Wikipedia, Individual Action on Climate Change
p92

Sciencing (19 April 2018) p92, 94

en.Wikipedia, KwaZulu-Natal p94

en.Wikipedia, Cape Town Water Crisis p96

Convention on Biological Diversity, What is Impact
Assessment? p103

Wilbrink & Associates ZA, Environmental Impact
Assessment p103

Land Survey Africa p105

Scientific American by Diana Kwon (20th May 2016)
p123

Index

Associated with Noah's Ark

£1 in every sale goes to the Foundation:

Dennis to Alice

GEORGE S BOUGHTON

PLANTS
&
US

How they shape
human history and society

John Akeroyd

Foreword by Sir Tim Smit